A New Approach to the Economics of Public Goods

Public goods are typically defined only in reference to the good itself but, as this book argues, the public goods can be better understood if contextual variables are incorporated. This book discusses the production and provision of public goods. It asserts that changes related to public goods are better understood if the category of goods are not decided solely by the properties of the good itself. We also need to focus on how the *enabled* utility of a good is influenced by the production and the provision of the good

The book opens with a brief introduction to common conceptions of public goods and a review of the existing literature – highlighting the limitations of current definitions of public goods. It presents a new multi-layered approach to public goods. This has implications for the discourse on public goods and for our understanding of the societal and environmental impact of public goods. The implications are illustrated in several areas; public goods in ancient history, privatization, innovation, competitiveness and prices, democracy and political standards, and economic growth.

The book provides a provocative argument for a new way to analyze public goods which will appeal to scholars and students interested in the economic analysis of public goods, arguments regarding the privatizing or nationalizing of production and services, and method of modelling and measuring sustainable business activities.

Thomas Laudal is Associate Professor of international business strategy at the University of Stavanger Business School, Norway.

Routledge Frontiers of Political Economy

For more information about this series, please visit: www.routledge.com/
books/series/SE0345

A New Approach to the Economics of Public Goods

Thomas Laudal

Routledge
Taylor & Francis Group

LONDON AND NEW YORK

First published 2020
by Routledge
2 Park Square, Milton Park, Abingdon, Oxon OX14 4RN

and by Routledge
52 Vanderbilt Avenue, New York, NY 10017

Routledge is an imprint of the Taylor & Francis Group, an informa business

© 2020 Thomas Laudal

British Library Cataloguing-in-Publication Data
A catalogue record for this book is available from the British Library

Library of Congress Cataloging-in-Publication Data
A catalog record for this book has been requested

ISBN: 978-0-367-32104-8 (hbk)
ISBN: 978-0-429-31661-6 (ebk)

Typeset in Times New Roman
by Apex CoVantage, LLC

Contents

Preface

There is a link between the *political* debate about public or private services and the *economic* debate about public goods. In line with much of the economic literature in this field, the premise of this book is that the debate on public goods does not decide whether services should be public or private. We know that many public goods (non-excludable and/or non-rival goods) are provided by private entities just as many private goods are provided by public entities. However, even though analysis of public goods is not in itself decisive with regard to the appropriate sector, understanding the key characteristics of public goods is critical for our preparation for this debate. It is asserted that a multi-layered approach to public goods is suited to qualify not only the excludability and rivalry of goods, but also the efficiency and sustainability related to the value-added process.

This book is inspired by discussions with colleagues at the University of Stavanger Business School and by debates I have been part of concerning private provision of education, health services, and other public services the last 15–20 years. Among the most noticeable features in these debates has been the lack of principles backing different viewpoints. This could be because the introduction of private services happens relatively slowly, without major reforms that has to be defended. It could also be because there is a growing proportion of the population that can afford privatized services in many areas, resulting in a greater focus on private benefits. Finally, the lack of principles backing viewpoints could be because we lack precise concepts and a consensus on how to define and delineate the relevant issues. The aim of this book is to offer a nuanced analysis of public goods by introducing more precise public good categories, and by relating these categories in a way that contribute to a better understanding of the competitive options available to businesses, and the most efficient and sustainable options available to governments.

Acknowledgements

The ideas behind this book has matured more than three years while I have been lecturing and participating in other projects. I need to thank many people for inspiring and guiding me along the way. Jan Erik Lane, professor emeritus at the University of Geneva, was one of the first who encouraged me in several emails commenting on early drafts. I am also grateful for the feedback and debates with my colleagues Gorm Kipperberg, Jonathan Muringani, and Ola Kvaløy. I am particularly grateful for the comments I received from Jan Tore Solstad at NTNU Business School at the last stages of this work. I also thank the three anonymous reviewers for corrections and advice, and Andy Humphries and Ajanta Bhattacharjee at Routledge for their excellent support. Finally, I thank my wife, Elise, our two young boys, Even and Amund, and my parents, Birgit and Arnfinn, for taking part in numerous discussions about public goods.

1 Introduction

This text addresses the production and provision of public goods. It asserts that changes related to public goods are better understood if the category of goods are not decided solely by the properties of the good itself.[1] Relevant elements external to the good itself are the positive and negative externalities generated during production and the manner in which the good is provided to users/consumers and how this affects their access to the good.

Properties related to the production and provision of a public good are included in many published studies, but they are typically treated as exogenous variables. When the category of a public good is decided only by referring to the good itself, we focus on the *potential* utility, or the *ideal* utility of the good. The argument here is that the analysis of public goods also needs to focus on how the *enabled* utility of a good is influenced by the production and the provision of the good. It is argued that the defining characteristics of public goods should incorporate contextual variables by distinguishing between three public good "layers":

- The utility-layer: The potential utility of the good itself.
- The supply-layer: The manner in which the good is provided.
- The conversion-layer: Characteristics of the value-added process.

We may consider arguments in favour of or against public goods by referring to the categories in the utility-layer and the supply-layer. We may further qualify public goods by characterizing the goods' transformation, or the value-added process related to the provision of the good, by referring to the conversion-layer.

We start with a brief introduction to common conceptions of public goods in the economic literature. Then we present examples of changes of public goods that are described by referring to the distinction between a utility-layer and a supply-layer. Thereafter we extend this model by adding a conversion-layer to further qualify the public good. The next chapters look into several cases that show the descriptive and predictive advantages of a multi-layered approach to public goods. Finally we discuss whether the multi-layered approach may help us to better understand trends regarding public goods.

Note

1 The reference to "goods" in this text is meant to capture natural resources, commodities, and services, and both monetized and non-monetized transactions. This is in line with the tradition, starting with Alfred Marshall, when "wealth" became a reference to both "material" and "immaterial" goods (Hill, 1999, p. 433).

2 The economic literature on public goods

Most studies of public goods consider public and private goods as opposites. It is common to refer to two dimensions; a "non-excludable/excludable" dimension, and a "non-rival/rival" dimension. Our current understanding of public goods is based on insights of such diverse authors as Samuelson (1954), Head (1962), Buchanan (1965), Hardin (1968), Musgrave and Musgrave (1973), Ostrom and Ostrom (1977), Cowen (1985), Cornes and Sandler (1996), and Ledyard (1994).

From early on, it was pointed out that management of a public good is difficult when the task is left to a large group. David Hume wrote in the "Treatise of Human Nature", first published in 1739:

> Two neighbours may agree to drain a meadow, which they possess in common; because it is easy for them to know each other's mind; and each must perceive that the immediate consequence of his failing in his part, is the abandoning the whole project. But it is very difficult, and indeed impossible, that a thousand persons should agree in any such action; it being difficult for them to concert so complicated a design, and still more difficult for them to execute it; while each seek a pretext to free himself of the trouble and expense, and would lay the whole burden on others.
>
> (Hume, 1888, p. 538)

Another example of an early mentioning of the challenge of managing public goods is a lecture by professor of political economy, W. F. Lloyd, published in 1832. Lloyd claimed that contributing to a collective good is challenging when the group is large due to diminishing returns:

> beyond a certain point of minuteness, the interest would be so small as to elude perception, and would obtain no hold whatever on the human mind.
>
> (Lloyd, 1832, p. 18)

The remedy to these types of cases are "political society", or "political associations",[1] according to Hume (1888, p. 538). Other scholars focus on services that are suitable for public administration. Here the main issue is not the challenges of collective governance, but which functions are fit for governance by state institutions. Cohn (1895, p. 144) is one. He claims there are four classes of services fit for public administration:

- Services offered to the individual in exchange for some kind of payment.
- Institutional services that cannot be subdivided.
- Services in exchange for payment but engaged by a group and payed for according to ability, not according to the benefits received.
- Services that are offered to support the needs of one or more classes of citizens.

Modern economists have attempted to express the general challenges related to how large groups consider and share public goods. Paul A. Samuelson is one of the pioneers in this field. A question posed by Samuelson (1954) was whether it is possible to calculate the optimal public expenditure by applying an econometric model. He started out with two categories of goods: "ordinary private consumption goods" and "collective consumption goods". In a formalized mathematical model, he demonstrates that an optimal public expenditure, defined as a Pareto efficient equilibrium, is not calculable in a decentralized market, or by voting mechanisms. According to Oakland (1969), Samuelson demonstrates how over- or under-production may lead to problems when we deal with both pure and impure public goods. It could be shown that pareto optimal conditions demand that public policy addresses the distribution of these goods (Oakland, 1969, p. 268). The distribution of public goods was addressed by Charles M. Tiebout in 1956. If consumers are mobile, we may see a large number of communities offering different *variants* of public goods.

> The consumer-voter may be viewed as picking the community which best satisfies his preference pattern for public goods.
>
> (Tiebout, 1956, p. 418)

It was assumed that there is an optimally sized community at each location. Consumers will sort themselves into homogenous communities offering the efficient amount of public goods. In these communities a Pareto efficient equilibrium, as described in Samuelson (1954), could be calculated in a decentralized market. It has been left to others to provide more detailed calculations and more realistic assumptions (Batina & Ihori,

2005, p. 311). According to Stiglitz (1982), Tiebout's conclusion only holds under very special and unreasonable assumptions.

Head (1962) elaborates on the results of Samuelson (1954), when he shows that the discussions on "jointness" and "excludability" of goods are unrelated. Richard Musgrave has since made major contributions in particular by synthesizing earlier contributions in the field (see Sturn, 2010), and Musgrave and Musgrave (1973) and Cornes and Sandler (1996) popularized these insights.

Buchanan (1965) focused on "club goods" which refer to collective goods where exclusion is possible. Later these were labelled "toll goods" in Ostrom and Ostrom (1977). Buchanan found that an optimal relationship between the good and the number of members in a club is calculable given there are certain rules for participation. A key implementation of this is to allow for more flexible property arrangements and to develop exclusion mechanisms. Musgrave and Musgrave (1973, pp. 53–54) summarized the reasons causing market failures of public goods in a table where four categories of goods were determined by two dichotomies "excludability"/"non-excludability" and "rival consumption"/"non-rival consumption".

Ostrom and Ostrom (1977) explored the question of how we ought to organize and manage collective goods in general. They referred to the nature of public goods by categorizing public goods in four quadrants determined by two dimensions, first presented in Musgrave and Musgrave (1973): *Excludability/non-excludability* and *joint/individual* (rival/non-rival). According to Ostrom and Ostrom (1977) empirical evidence show that small groups and individuals are more successful in providing public goods than large groups.[2] This is why people seek governmental institutions. However, government distribution (bureaucracy) could lead to tyranny and difficulties in measuring performance, and a lack of communication between production units and consumers. Ostrom and Ostrom (1977) suggested that public goods are manageable when collective consumption is organized apart from production, and when we apply a market-like arrangement among producers and collective consumption units. This has been viewed as a "third way" apart from private and government property and has received much criticism (Block & Jankovic, 2016).

In the popular text by Hardin (1968), the prerequisites for a sustainable management of commons is discussed. A "commons" is exemplified by a plot of land used for grazing by a herd of livestock. According to Hardin, the rational individual will add animals to the herd to expand their activity, and thereby to increase their revenue. However, this will lead to the soil being depleted, and threaten the livelihood of all. Hardin (1968) claims that the history of human collaboration shows that commons are being abandoned in area after area. He claims that collective management of a commons only succeeds under conditions of low population-density. This view was challenged by scholars (e.g. Ostrom, 1990; Solstad & Brekke, 2011). A common argument is that the capacity of individuals to extricate themselves from various types of dilemmas related to common pool goods is contingent on the institutional environment and that there are many examples of this. Referring to Hardin (1968), Ostrom described a game in which the livestock owners can succeed in making a binding contract to commit themselves to a cooperative strategy that they themselves work out. Based on a number of case studies, Ostrom (1990, p. 90) suggested there are eight design principles that characterize a robust management of a common pool resource. These governance principles ensure broad participation in the governance of these resources and predictability and risk mitigation for the participants.[3] Solstad and Brekke (2011) show that a pareto-optimal Nash equilibrium[4] is achieved in a context where rational individuals manage a common pool resource, modelled as a two-stage sequential game. First, the harvesting of renewable natural resources takes place. Then the surplus from this stage is used for buying private goods and contributing to public goods. In this setting it is shown that the individuals share the objective of maximizing the total surplus.

In experiment studies, a public good is typically regarded as a collective asset managed by voluntary contributions. These studies include different setups involving participants contributing to the asset in the experiment. Central questions are whether people are more or less cooperative or selfish, and what the factors are that influence their willingness to pay for a good. Experiment studies show how participation and attitudes depend on different design factors surrounding the experiment (Ledyard, 1994), e.g. how the participants' cooperation is improved when certain social norms are internalized (e.g. Rege & Telle, 2004). Other studies show that the willingness to pay for a public good cannot always be calculated by aggregating units belonging to a more general category (e.g. linked to territory or time). If a private purchase of the good is conceivable, as in the case of access to fishing resources for example, we tend to see aggregated values more frequently than if private purchasing of the good is unconceivable, as in the case of air traffic controls (Kahneman & Knetsch, 1992).

In general, most of the economic literature on public goods focus on the optimal distribution and the optimal price, and on problems related to collective governance. There is some agreement among economists on the difficulties involved in calculating the optimal expenditure of a public good. And several social scientists are critical to the mere notion that we are able to calculate or govern public goods by referring only to properties of the good itself. According to Cowen (1985) we need to include the institutional framework surrounding the good, and how the good is produced and provided to determine the category of the public good. Stretton and Orchard (1994) argue that the amount and kind of public goods in mixed economies must be ordered and allocated by a mixture of political, administrative, and market choices. Majority rule – directly at the political level, or indirectly at the administrative level – should influence the amount and kind of public goods, not only markets. Malkin and Wildavsky (1991) also believe the institutional and political framework should influence the public good category, but they underline that efforts to categorize public goods are, and must be, a normative exercise; public goods are socially constructed.

Neither of these critiques present a model which incorporates characteristics of both the good itself, and the relevant institutional framework, though they take the position that institutional or political contexts should be recognized when the type of public good is determined. Cowen (1985) points to the lack of institutional variables in such analysis, Stretton and Orchard (1994) argue that elected entities should have a say, while Malkin and Wildavsky (1991) dismiss the notion that we should look for discrete criteria determining public goods categories.

The aim of the multi-layered approach to public goods is to meet the critique of the institutionalists, the levellers, and the social constructivists by suggesting a model that incorporates the main features of the good itself *and* the relevant institutional framework.

Notes

1 In the 18th century the term "society" commonly referred to as an association of persons, not to the more general notion of a "community". Hence, today we should probably understand this reference as a reference to "an association with a political purpose or aim" (Online Etymology Dictionary: www.etymon line.com/word/society).
2 'The linking of group size and "public good" dates back to the writings of the ancient philosophers in Greece. Aristotle declared that order could be achieved only in a place small enough for everyone to hear the herald's cry and that an excessively large number cannot participate in order' (Hayek 1988:45)."
3 The eight principles in Ostrom (1990, p. 90): 1) clearly defined boundaries, 2) congruence between appropriation and provision rules, 3) collective choice arrangements, 4) monitoring, 5) graduated sanctions, 6) conflict resolutions mechanisms, 7) recognition of rights to organize, and 8) for common pool goods that are part of larger systems, the seven first principles should be taken care of by a multi-level governance framework.
4 A pareto-optimal Nash equilibrium is a solution to a non-cooperative game with two or more players, where the allocation of resources is such that it is impossible to reallocate and make any one individual better off without making at least one individual worse off.

3 Advantages of studying public goods with reference to a utility-layer and a supply-layer

Public good dimensions and categories

When studies attempt to decompose public goods they normally refer to an excludability dimension and a rivalry dimension (Musgrave & Musgrave, 1973; Ostrom & Ostrom, 1977).[1] It is common, in particular in introductory textbooks in Economics, to distinguish between four goods:

Table 3.1 Public goods: The four quadrants.

	Jointness	*Rival*
Non-excludability	*1 Shared**	*2 Common pool*
Excludability	*4 Toll*	*3 Private*

* Joint, non-excludable goods are here labelled "shared goods", not "public goods" as in Ostrom and Ostrom (1977)[2]

The four quadrants in the public goods table refer to two dimensions where both non-excludability and jointness may be interpreted as market failures (Lane, 1993, p. 23). Scholars agree that most public goods in real life are "impure". They resemble, more or less, one of the public goods categories. It is also a common understanding that we should not treat the dimensions as continuous. There is neither a continuum between perfect competition and monopoly, nor between government provision of goods and market provision of goods (Cornes & Sandler, 1996, p. 9).[3] There are various variables separating the extremes in the two dimensions. And "jointness" may indicate "low rivalry", but it may also indicate that the good may not easily be partitioned. Though it is not always true that "jointness"-"rival" define a common dimension,[4] we shall try to expand our understanding of public goods as "categories" or "positions" in two-dimensional matrices, as this seems to be useful when we discuss the technological, economic, and institutional options linked to a change in the public good category. Showing public goods in quadrants in a matrix suggests that public goods are categories within a *system*. An alternative approach is to state that public goods are goods where there is a publicly recognized *need* as proposed by Light (2000). This means that public goods are defined by the subjective perception of those using/consuming the goods and will vary between cultures, societies, and different economic welfare levels. A variant of this is merit goods. These goods should benefit the users/consumers even in situations where they are not in demand by the targeted customer/consumer group. Musgrave and Musgrave (1973) characterized the incentives or subsidies promoting such kind of goods to the less affluent as an expression of paternalism. The aim is to correct the market in situations where users/consumers lack relevant information. In the present text the need, or merit, is not referred to as a defining characteristic of a public good.

The basic concepts describing public goods

"Goods": Refers to anything that is in demand by humans

In a wider understanding, "a good" is defined as anything that is good, or something that has economic utility, or satisfies an economic want (Webster dictionary). We refer to "users/consumers" in contexts where the public good may be a commodity, service, or something consumable.

1) "Shared goods": A good where there is joint and uninhibited access

A "shared good" is shared in two ways: First, *the nature of the good* demands that the good is shared among those demanding the good. There is an uninhibited access to the good and it is not possible for companies to appropriate the *full* benefits arising from their production or distribution of the good. Second; it must also be shared in order to be *fully utilized*: To benefit from the good it must be utilized by a group. "Shared" is associated with something owned, divided, felt, or experienced by more than one person (Cambridge.org), or *as* something we have in common, or held or experienced in common (thefreedictionary.com).

2) "Common pool": An aggregate good to be utilized by individuals

A "pool" is defined as a number of people or a quantity of a particular thing, such as money, collected together for shared use by several people or organizations (Cambridge.org). It may also refer to an aggregation of the interests or property of different persons made to further a joint undertaking by subjecting them to the same control and a common liability (merriam-webster.com).

> *3) "Toll"*: **A good where individuals have a right to utilize but not to own**
>
> It may be local authorities granting a right or a privilege (Dictionary. com). It may be the right to use roads, bridges, etc. in exchange for a fee to cover the cost of maintenance and depreciation (Dictionary. com).
>
> *4) "Private"*: **A good where access is reserved to one or more individual actors**
>
> We associate private with anything intended for, or restricted to, the use of a particular person, group, or class, or belonging to, or concerning, an individual person, company, or interest (Merriam-webster.org).

Many scholars insist that "pure public goods" ("shared goods" in Table 3.1) are only those commodities/services that are both non-excludable (it is not possible to stop others from enjoying it) and non-rivalrous (one person's consumption does not reduce other's potential consumption). An example of this is Lester Thurow's treatment of public goods in *The future of capitalism* (1996). After a standard description of public goods, he concludes:

> Education and health care certainly don't qualify. Individuals do not share their education or health care with anyone else, and those who don't pay . . . can be excluded.
>
> (Thurow, 1996, pp. 272–273)

This claim rests on the assumption that the public good category should be determined by focusing on the good itself, without considering how it is provided. In this example hospital treatment in itself is obviously a private good. However, the *provision* of hospital services in Scandinavia and in the United Kingdom, knowing that hospitals are financed by taxes and provided by the state, have characteristics which transforms the private good (the good itself) to a non-excludable good:

- The many advanced competences required to run a modern hospital must benefit a large group to be utilized effectively. And since the education of hospital employees is largely funded by taxpayers, hospital services depend on all citizens contributing their resources.

- The significant capital investments involved in the construction of a modern hospital, means that it has to benefit a large group to be utilized effectively. And since these investments are funded, or significantly subsidized, by tax payers, hospitals would not exist without citizens both contributing and benefitting from them.
- The core function of hospitals – to prioritize patients based on the severity of their health problems – requires hospitals to practice a non-discriminatory system of admission.

When we consider this *provision* of public hospital services, we see that it is non-excludable and both rivalrous and non-rivalrous: The characteristics of a non-excludable public good are needed in order to operate as a publicly provided service. This shows that it is helpful to distinguish between the good itself and the provision of the good in order to understand the role of public goods in society. This distinction is illustrated in Figure 3.1.

In what follows, the case is made for a split between a supply-layer and a utility-layer in order to better understand issues related to public goods, including the implications of the growing complexity of modern supply chains for public goods. The split will demonstrate that changing positions in the utility-layer are mostly due to changes in technology, while changes in the supply-layer are mostly due to organizational and policy-related changes. An example of this is when a new technical design (referring to the utility-layer) is made public for all to see and utilize, but where the patent system temporarily transforms this design into a private good (referring to the supply-layer). Kaul (2010) refers to patented knowledge as "global public goods with restricted access". And when John Kenneth

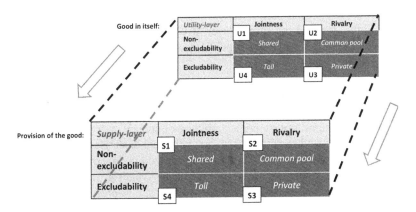

Figure 3.1 Distinguishing between a supply-layer and a utility-layer.

Galbraith addresses the distinction between private and social goods he refers to the organizational and policy-related changes:

> The line between public and private activity . . . is the product of many forces; tradition, ideological preference, social urgency, and political convenience all play a part.
>
> (Galbraith, 1958, p. 241)

Thus, the provision of the public good influence the public good category. We find that changes in the goods' position in the utility-layer are less frequent than the position in the supply-layer. Doering (2007) points out that services provided by democratic states change, depending on the governing alliances forming after each election. Thus, in democracies, the range of public goods varies over time, even without significant shifts of technology or significant organizational innovations.

It is also clear that the supply-layer is only meaningful for goods provided by *humans* while the utility-layer may also cover goods with no direct human involvement like sunsets, mountain-views, or natural hot springs.

Finally, we will see that the utility-layer characterizes the *potential* utility, or the *ideal* utility, related to a good, while the supply-layer describes the *enabled* utility related to the organizational design and policies influencing how goods are provided and accessed. Kaul and Mendoza (2003) make the distinction between "goods that have a potential for being public" and "de facto public goods". De facto goods are goods as they appear after public policy choices have decided how the goods are to be provided. Policy decisions may change the original category of the good. Kaul and Mendoza use this distinction in analysis of global public goods in international relations, but not as generic categories for any kind of public good.

Before we look into how we determine the position of a public good in the utility-layer and the supply-layer, it is helpful to consider incentives contributing to the provision of public goods.

Selective incentives contributing to the provision of public goods

In all large organizations there is a mixture of collective goals at the organizational level and private goals at the individual level. Building on work describing free-riding and the prisoners' dilemma in collective action problems (e.g. Alexander Hamilton and James Madison in the late 18th century), Mancur Olson (1971) questions how a non-profit organization, with collective goals of a kind that resemble a public good when they are achieved, is able to attract large numbers of members (Dougherty, 2003).

Olson compares this to similar market contexts. It is broadly accepted that markets are unable to restrain their production volume in order to attain the optimal return of the market as a hole without an external input. When individual companies in a market maximize their potential income, market prices may fall and lead to a suboptimal revenue for the market as a hole. Similarly, in large organizations it is a challenge to retain the optimal collective good. That is, to attract all the members that would benefit from achieving the organization's collective goals. This is due to the fact that individual actions often are unnoticeable in large organizations: It does not affect their share of the good achieved by the organization whether they participate or free-ride. In other words, it is difficult to reserve the public good obtained by the organization for any sub-group of users. Therefore, the organization needs to put in place incentives to attract and retain members. The nation-state needs compulsory taxes to finance public goods. Large non-profit organizations aiming for public goods need incentives distinct from the public good associated with the organization to attract members. It could be a reduced insurance premium, gadgets, or a newsletter offered only to members. The claim that large non-profit organizations' dependence on added or "selective" incentives to attract members is today a commonly accepted element of the operation of such organizations. We see this in literature reviews addressing selective incentives, or benefits, that are most effective in mobilizing support (e.g. Knoke, 1988; Chinman & Wandersman, 1999), and in more recent publications on the sharing economy and the level of resources able to incentivize members in organizations (e.g. Hira & Reilly, 2017).

The general question addressed by this literature is why people invest time and money to be part of organizations that, on the surface, seem only to offer non-excludable goods. In this text we do not deal with the question of why people join organizations or how organizations are able to achieve their potential. We attempt to qualify public goods, and in particular focus on how the number of potential and actual beneficiaries vary according to the provision of the good. The aim is to use a distinction between three "layers"; the good itself (the utility-layer), the provision of the good (the supply-layer), and the value-added process (the conversion layer), to better understand how technological, economic, and institutional trends affect the characteristics of public goods and vice-versa. This is in line with Gerhard Colm who criticized Paul A. Samuelson for reducing our expression of preferences to only two measures, through the market mechanism (private goods) and through the ballot-box (public goods):

> We need a corresponding notion of the political decision-making process in which government functionaries, economic organisations,

and individuals play a role. With respect to the role of individuals in the political decisions, Samuelson's concept does not appear to me to be useful.

(Colm, 1956, p. 409)

The decision-making process and institutional contexts are highlighted when we distinguish between public goods in a utility-layer – categorizing the good itself – and in a supply-layer – categorizing the provision of the good.

Determining the position of a public good in the utility-layer and the supply-layer

The utility-layer ("U")

How do we characterize the public good by determining the good's position in the utility-layer (see Figure 3.1)? We need to consider the following question: What characterizes the utility of the good itself with regard to the dimensions "jointness/rivalry" and "excludability"?

Jointness/rivalry dimension

The typical feature of a good characterized by "jointness" is that, once it is available, it is equally available to all (Head, 1962, p. 201). These goods have negligible marginal cost coupled with a capacity constraint (Davis, 1967, p. 368), and they are "non-subtractable" (Ostrom, 1977, p. 5). On this background, the following two questions are suited to determine the position on the jointness/rivalry dimension in the utility-layer:

• Is the good part of a common resource base where we observe elements of a zero sum game? ("Yes" indicates rivalry) If the good is abundant, and low-cost, there are weak incentives for rival behaviour among users/customers.
• Is the good that people are seeking non-subtractable? ("Yes" indicates jointness) Is the nature of the good such that it may be partitioned? ("Yes" indicates rivalry).

Excludability dimension

Public goods have traditionally been associated with goods that are not "marketable" (Adams & McCormick, 1987). However, it is clear that joint goods may be marketable. Both joint goods and rivalled goods may allow exclusion. We should then determine the position of non-excludable or excludable dimension in the utility-layer by asking two questions:

- Can those benefiting from the good be restricted to a selected group? ("Yes" indicates excludable.)
- Is the good suited for a market-based transactions, allowing supply and demand to determine prices? ("Yes" indicates excludable.)

When the goods are externalized beyond certain levels it is referred to as non-excludable. When a good is internalized beyond certain levels, it is referred to as excludable. This is not a reference to the externalities arising from the processing or recycling of the good, but to what we refer to as externalization of the good itself.

The supply-layer ("S")

When we are to determine the position in the supply-layer, the basic question is how the provision of the good, or the manner in which the good is offered, affects the extent of "jointness/rivalry" and "excludability". This is of interest because when there is rivalry among suppliers, or the provision of the good excludes certain users/consumers, this affects users' and/ or consumers' access to the good.

The competitive relationship among suppliers include the manner in which they favour certain customers. Thus, when we refer to rivalry and excludability as an element in the provision of goods, it is likely that certain users'/consumers' access to the goods are affected. Thus, rivalry and excludability due to the mode of supply of goods affects rivalry and excludability among users and consumers of goods. We will now consider how we may determine the position of public goods in the supply-layer.

Jointness/rivalry dimension

The following questions are proposed in order to determine the position on the jointness/rivalry dimension in the supply-layer:

- Questions to determine *jointness/rivalry* in the supply-layer, from the *suppliers'* perspective:
  - Are the suppliers of this good competing for the same customers?

    ("Yes" indicates rivalry). Opposite example: Providers of domestic household services typically compete for local employers,

> though there is a national market for domestic household services.

- Are the suppliers of this good threatened by new entrants or by suppliers of a substitute? ("Yes" indicates rivalry). Opposite example: State-owned and -operated hospitals are not subject to as strong competitive forces.

A positive answer to these question would refer to situations where firms within and industry put pressure on one another and limit each other's profit potential. The two questions cover the horizontal competition, or "forces" driving competition in Porter (1980).[5]

- Questions to determine jointness/rivalry in the supply-layer, from the *users' and consumers'* perspective:

  - Is there only a need for a basic fixed quantity per user/consumer of this good, and are there few options for differentiation? ("Yes" indicates low rivalry.) Example: Providers of electricity through a traditional power grid.
  - Is there relatively little need for suppliers to differentiate because the good addresses a basic human need? ("Yes" indicates low rivalry.) Example: Dental services have these characteristics.

We see "low rival supply" when there is inelastic demand,[6] that is, when the demand is relatively unaffected by purchasing power, or when there are few options for suppliers to influence the demand by differentiating the good.

Excludability dimension

Questions that are suited to determine the position on the excludability dimension in the supply-layer:

- Does the manner in which the good is provided systematically favour certain sub-groups within a similar need category? ("Yes" indicates excludability.) This could be because the manner in which the good is supplied, or it could be because the volume of supply does not satisfy the demand. When either of these circumstances hold, we see the supply affecting the user's access to the good. Example: Privately funded hospitals may exclude those that cannot afford particular treatments.
- Is the favouring of certain sub-groups not feasible because the unit price is close to nil? ("Yes" indicates non-excludability.) Example: Machine translation of text on the web (Boitet, Blanchon, Seligman, & Bellynck, 2010; Tufis, 2014).

The two questions concerning excludability addresses whether the good is offered in a manner which restricts sub-groups within a similar need category access to the good.

Summing up the positions in the supply-layer and utility-layer

The position in the utility-layer is determined by whether people may derive utility from the good collectively, or whether the utility is only attainable individually. The position in the utility-layer is also determined by whether the good can be divided and allocated in shares to individual users (excludable), or if the good is non-subtractable (rendering the exclusion difficult). The position of a good in the utility-layer may be changed when new technologies change the good's inherent properties.

The position in the supply-layer is determined by the manner in which the good is offered. Thus, the supply categories are typically determined by the organizational choices and policies influencing the provision of the good. This means that the position in the supply-layer are more dynamic than the position in the utility-layer. In Table 3.2 the position in the utility-layer expresses *the potential* utility of the good, while the position in the supply-layer expresses the *enabled* utility.

Several debates concerning public goods would benefit from distinguishing between the good itself and the provision of a good. Two examples illustrate this: First, we consider Ronald H. Coase's argument that lighthouses are mistakenly referred to as the prime example of a public good (Coase, 1974). Then we consider the claim made by J. Malkin and A. Wildavsky that the boundaries between public and private goods are essentially socially constructed (Malkin & Wildavsky, 1991). In the case presented by Coase (1974), it is not contested that the lighthouse service in itself is a non-rivalrous and non-excludable good (position "U1" in the utility layer), but Coase argues that the manner in which the service in many years was *provided* by private owners for a profit shows that this really is a private good (occupying position "S3" in the supply layer). In the case of Malkin and Wildavsky (1991) it is shown how a distinction between the nature of the good itself and the provision of the good, better prepare us for considering whether goods should be provided by public or private institutions.

Coase (1974) starts by referring to works by John Stuart Mill and Henry Sidgwick, and Arthur Cecil Pigou. These scholars have all mentioned lighthouses as an archetypical example of a public good. Coase also cites Paul A. Samuelson (1964) who argued that the zero marginal costs of additional ships using lighthouses, made it impossible to finance the service by a market-determined price, and that the social benefits of a

Table 3.2 Summarizing the criteria deciding the position in the utility- and the supply-layer

PUBLIC GOODS IN THE UTILITY-LAYER AND THE SUPPLY-LAYER		
Tendency	*General criteria*	*Specific criteria*
The utility-layer The *potential* utility derived from the good itself.		
DIMENSION 01: JOINTNESS/RIVALRY		
TENDENCY: RIVALRY	We see a zero-sum collection of goods and/or a subtractable good	UL/R1: The good is part of a limited common resource base UL/R2: The good may be partitioned
DIMENSION 02: EXCLUDABILITY		
TENDENCY: EXCLUDABLE	It is possible to restrict the number of beneficiaries	UL/E1: Beneficiaries of the good may be restricted to a selected group UL/E2: The price of the good may be determined by supply and demand in a market
The supply-layer The *enabled* utility derived from the provision of the good.		
DIMENSION 01: JOINTNESS/RIVALRY		
TENDENCY: RIVALRY	*Supplier perspective:* The market structure stimulates rivalry	SL/R/S1: Suppliers are competing for the same customers SL/R/S2: Suppliers are threatened by new entrants or substitutes
	User/consumer perspective: The demand is elastic	SL/R/U1: The demand is not restricted to a fixed quantity/quality SL/R/U2: The demand is not linked to a basic human need
DIMENSION 02: EXCLUDABILITY		
TENDENCY: EXCLUDABLE	Subgroups within the same need category are favoured	SL/E1: The good offered in a way that favours, or adapts to, the needs of certain subgroups SL/E2: The unit price of the good is not close to nil

"UL" = Utility layer. "SL" = Supply layer. "R" = Rivalry. "E" = Excludable. "U" = User/consumer perspective. "S" = Supplier-perspective.

lighthouse might well defend a mechanism that makes the service optimally available to all. Coase disagrees with all four authors. According to Coase, it is useful to consider the history of lighthouses if we want to consider whether the lighthouse services resemble a public good or not. The institution given the authority to govern lighthouses in the United Kingdom, originated from a seamen's guild probably sometime before the 14th century. In the middle of the 16th century the administration of seamarks was included as one of its privileges. The first lighthouses appeared early in the 17th century. A substantial part of the lighthouses (approximately 50 percent) were run by private parties during this first phase, according to Coase. In 1836 the Parliament decided that all lighthouses should be governed by public authorities and this was accomplished in 1842. The main arguments used in public discourse concerning lighthouses was that public ownership promised greater efficiency and the prospects of lower light fees when private profit was eliminated. It was showed in several reports after 1842 that the light fees were reduced. The system was also simplified, and the model in place in 1898 was still, in principle, the same as the current model at the time Coase wrote his paper.

The main point made by Coase is twofold. First, contrary to the references made by Mill, Sidgwick, and Pigou, history shows that it *is* possible to operate lighthouses privately for a profit.[7] Second, the viewpoint Coase ascribes to Samuelson – that the optimal solution would be to finance lighthouses by a general tax – is said to *reduce* the efficiency because the government would manage the system in a centralized manner, reducing the influence of users and managers of lighthouses who have the most relevant knowledge about how to maintain and develop systems for maritime navigation.

Whether we agree with the viewpoints of Coase or not is not the issue here.[8] The point is that the differences between Coase and the adversaries he selects concern the *provision* of "lighthouse services", not the properties of the lighthouse *service itself.* In the 120 years that have elapsed between the first and last publication referred to by Coase (between J. S. Mill and P. A. Samuelson), the technologies, organizational models, and policies for maritime transport and communications changed dramatically. The reason lighthouses are so popular in publications about public goods is that the good itself clearly satisfies the criterion of a non-excludable and non-rivalrous good. Beams of light are visible for all ships passing through the sector of the lighthouse. What has changed, and is changing continuously, is the policies and systems influencing the *provision* of this good. John Stuart Mill could not have envisioned an option for monitoring ship traffic the way Paul A. Samuelson suggested – by radar reconnaissance. And Ronald H. Coase did not foresee lighthouses being substituted by basic services in automated satellite communication systems where exclusion and rivalry is virtually non-existent. Today, it is still fair to characterize lighthouse services as a shared good in the utility-layer when we describe the potential utility linked to the product itself, after the development of technologies and governing systems the last centuries have changed the manner in which the lighthouse services are provided. The centralized supply, the nature of the demand, and the non-excludable nature of lighthouse services suggest that this is a shared supply ("S1"). However, when light fees were enforced on passing ships by private lighthouses, chances were that the suppliers attempted to differentiate among subgroups of users in order to maximize profits. In this period, we could say that if the private supply of lighthouse services became excludable, they occupied the position of a toll supply ("S3").

J. Malkin and A. Wildavsky criticize economists for using a definition of public goods that rests on the inherent properties of the good itself (Malkin & Wildavsky, 1991).[9] They argue that it is not possible to locate goods that have inherent properties which make them best suited for government provision. We should rather discuss what kind of goods we believe *ought* to be financed publicly. The position of Malkin and Wildavsky (1991) seems to equate analysis of whether technology and social organization influence goods' excludability and jointness/rivalry, or not, with political discussions about whether a good *should* be provided by the public or private sector. However, one of the most important advantages of discussing the status of public goods seems to be omitted. Joint and non-rivalrous goods may be subject to market forces (e.g. entrance to national parks and monuments or domestic household services). And there may be political consensus among all political factions that an excludable good should be provided by the government (e.g. hospital treatment and equipment for handicapped persons in Scandinavia). If we did not have precise concepts developed for the specific purpose of analyzing the nature and provision of goods, we would be left with a debate about "private or government provision" – a discourse which often becomes superficial without considering the nature of public goods. We would lack the insights needed for debating how we should manage natural and economic resources, the market structure, and the interface between public and private institutions in addition to the preferred solution regarding possible private or public funding and management.

Examples of changes referring to the utility-layer zand the supply-layer

Examples of how public goods change with new technologies, organization models, and policies may be viewed as changing trajectories over time within, and between, the utility-layer and the supply-layer (Figure 3.1).

To get a better understanding of the multi-layered approach to public goods let us consider the following four examples.

Example 1: Growing turnover of private hospitals

Hospitals offer clinical treatments and care. This good is "consumed" individually and patients are often in a position to choose the hospital where they would like to be treated. This good, therefore, permits rivalry in the utility-layer. It is also possible to exclude groups and individuals within the same need category. Thus, hospital services fit the category "private good" in the utility-layer.

What public good category does hospital services fit in the *supply* layer? *Public* hospitals are often part of a large and dominant healthcare unit in a local or regional community, experiencing relatively weak competitive pressures. The services of public hospitals are normally not part of an environment that inspires rivalrous behaviour. It is not provided as an excludable service. Public health services do not favour sub-groups within similar need categories. Public hospitals' responsibility is, at least for basic services, to offer treatment to all residents within a geographic area, and patients are only charged a sum that is stipulated in state regulations. The range of services and capacity is defined by a number of specialists with competences based on many years of public education and training. Thus, public hospital services have many features in common with "common pool supply" ("S2"), and with a "shared supply" ("S1"). *Private* hospitals are funded by patients' direct payment, by out-of-pocket insurance, and by employer-covered insurance schemes. They experience relative strong commercial pressures, and though they depend on government approval and public education for qualifying healthcare employees, we see rivalry. They compete for patients and for qualified specialists. The different price models offered to the public cover different symptoms and illnesses and different guaranteed response times. Thus, private hospitals favour subgroups within the same need-category. We see that private hospital care shows characteristics of rivalry *and* excludability, and therefore fits the category of a private supply ("S3").

We see that hospital care is a private good in the utility-layer ("U3"). While it is partly a common pool supply ("S2") and partly a shared supply ("S1") when it is offered by a *public* hospital, and a private supply ("S3") when it is offered by a *private* actor for profit.

In many countries, the growth in the turnover of private hospital care is much higher than the growth in public hospitals. Statistics from the OECD (Health Expenditure Indicators), show that many countries in Europe and the Americas (Belgium, Czech Republic, Denmark, France, Portugal,

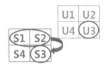

Figure 3.2 Changing positions in Figure 3.1: A growing private hospital sector.

Slovenia, Iceland, USA, Canada, and Mexico) have seen more than a 120 percent real growth in their out-of-pocket insurance and employer-based insurance schemes for hospital care between 2000 and 2015 (OECD, 2017a). The inflation, based on food prices in the same period, is between 20 and 40 percent (OECD, 2017b). Thus, it is likely that we see a partial shift from "S1"/"S2" to S3" in the supply-layer for hospital services in many countries. Later we will see that the shift from "S2" to "S3" for private goods ("U3") also can be related to increasing differences in purchasing power.

The growth of private hospital care may be described as a change in the provision of a private good ("U3") from a shared supply and common pool supply ("S1"/"S2") to a private supply ("S3") (Table 3.2).

Example 2: Growing turnover of private universities

Being a student at a university means that you enjoy a good that depends on the participation of relatively large groups of likeminded people. The university facilities (buildings, labs, etc.), education, and research depend on *groups* of students, administrators, and professors working together to achieve the required quality and capacity. The learning outcome depends on students engaging with each other. By socializing and competing for grades they stimulate each other, and in colloquiums and group assignments and mutual learning. Thus, the University offers a joint good to students. Rival behaviour, understood as behaviour where someone is competing for a piece of a common resource base, or competing for the same share of a good, is not characteristic of the good "university education". However, the admission criteria, and the grading which decides whether students are admitted or not, show that university education is an excludable good.[10] Thus, university education seems to be a joint and excludable good and therefore have the hallmarks of a toll good ("U4") in the utility-layer.

One of the important differences between private and public universities is the different tuition levels[11] (OECD, 2017c). In many OECD countries, the average tuition fee at private universities are more than double the

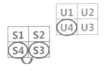

Figure 3.3 Changing positions in Figure 3.1: A growing turnover of private universities.

average tuition fees at public universities.[12] In countries where the tuition levels at public universities are very low, universities do not favour sub-groups within the same need-category. But students are favoured based on their academic merits as this is part of the core purpose of the university. Thus, the good offered by public universities that only charge a minimal tuition have characteristics of a toll supply ("S4"). The higher tuition levels at private universities suggests that these universities favour sub-groups within the same academic need-category, that is, within student groups with similar performance levels. The education offered by private universities therefore resemble a private supply ("S3").

Government approved statistics shows that private expenditure on higher education institutions generally increased faster than public expenditure between 2000 and 2012. The average share of public funding for higher education institutions in the OECD area decreased from 69 percent in 2000 to 64 percent in 2012.[13] The growth of private universities may be described as a change of a toll good ("U4") in the utility-layer, from a common pool supply ("S2") to a private supply ("S3") in the supply-layer[14] (Figure 3.3).

Example 3: Hotels losing market shares to online accommodation sharing

Accommodation services allow for rivalry and are subtractable in the sense that those who offer accommodation may vary the scale of the service from only a few beds, to thousands. In addition, the great variation in price ranges shows that accommodation services are excludable. Thus, the accommodation services should be considered a private good ("U3") in the utility-layer.

The provision of accommodation services by hotels is generally considered a highly competitive market. Both in local and international markets we see a mix of minor actors and large dominant actors. Accommodation services are differentiated from the most luxurious and lavish experiences to the stripped down and shabby. Thus, the provision of hotel services are rivalrous and excludable and may be considered as a private good ("S3") in the supply-layer.

Today, the hotel businesses' share of the accommodation market is challenged by the growth of online peer-to-peer (P2P) accommodation services. One of the dominant P2P actors in the global market is Airbnb. Since the launch in 2008, Airbnb does not own any of the accommodations it offers on its website. It has developed a platform and a website where private hosts and private guests meet. Its role is to facilitate. It does not take responsibility for cleaning services, for training the hosts, for vetting the guests, or for insurance needs.[15] Its main revenue source is the service fee of 3 percent charged on each reservation. Reservations are based on the pictures and texts submitted by private hosts, read by people searching the Airbnb website. According to information published by Airbnb (www.airbnb.com) in 2017/2018, they had more than 300,000 listings in 65,000 cities in 191 countries.

The P2P accommodation services, facilitated by Airbnb, are based on owners of private dwellings who's property value represent only a small fraction of the relevant accommodation market, and they experience limited competitive pressure. There is also little differentiation of the products; Airbnb does not differentiate between hosts, and owners who offer dwellings on Airbnb do not typically differentiate between guests the way hotels do. Thus, the P2P accommodation service of Airbnb show few characteristics of rival supply. When it comes to excludability, hosts of the P2P accommodation service may favour whoever they want as guests by selecting a particular pricing model, and by vetting the requests they receive. Thus, this P2P accommodation service show the characteristics of an excludable supply. Being excludable, but less rivalrous, the P2P accommodation service of Airbnb may be characterized as a toll supply ("S4").

The market share of Airbnb compared to the hotel business in Europe increased from less than 2 percent in 2012 to 6 percent in 2015.[16] Studies show an increase of market shares in Amsterdam from 5.4 percent in 2015 to 10.7 percent in 2016 (Tourism Review, 2017), and in Reykjavik from 20 percent in 2015 to 40 percent in 2016 (Landsbankinn Economic Research, 2017). The volume of online home sharing services (e.g. Airbnb, HomeAway, and Couchsurfing) was estimated to represent 9 percent of the traditional hotel market in the western world in 2014, and Airbnb bookings were predicted to grow from 10 million bookings in 2015 to 60 million booking in by 2020 (Saussier, 2015). This increase of market shares from online services may be described as a change in the position of a public good in the supply-layer from a private supply ("S3") to a toll supply ("S4") (Figure 3.4).

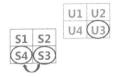

Figure 3.4 Changing positions in Figure 3.1: A growing market share of online accommodation sharing services.

Example 4: Smart grids substituting traditional power grids

Companies producing electric power do not target individuals or small groups when they offer their products. Significant investments, both in power generation facilities and in distribution and transforming capacities, necessitates that electricity is offered to large groups, normally to anyone connected to the grid. Individual customers in this large group do not experience a zero sum game; the consumption of one does not reduce the consumption of others. Thus, the traditional power grid and power generation is a joint good. When you offer electricity to all households connected to a grid, it is not practical to restrict their physical access to electricity to subgroups. However, meters linked to different tariffs exclude customers based on what they can afford. Therefore, electricity generation and distribution are excludable goods in the sense that it is fit for market-based transactions. Being both a joint good and an excludable good, the traditional electricity distribution therefore may be labelled toll goods in the utility-layer ("U4").

Electricity suppliers typically have a substantial share of their local market. This is true not only for companies controlling distribution and transmission where it is not possible to have many grids in parallel, but also for the service offered by companies generating electrical power, or by companies with a trade license (Nepal & Jamasb, 2015). In a highly regulated market, where supplying entities need substantial investments to control power generation and/or distribution, competitive pressures are tempered. This suggests that there is limited rival behaviour among the suppliers in this industry. But electricity providers are differentiating their product by offering different price models. Given that the supply of electricity is less rivalrous, and excludable due to price differentiation, this good may be labelled a toll supply ("S4").

The introduction of an advanced grid management systems, based on an exchange of electricity among a large group of generators and consumers, supported by broad band communication technology and internet of things, will influence the nature of this public good. The term "smart grid" refers to the future model of the power grid. There is consensus among many scholars that "smart grid" refers to four unique features (e.g. Brown, 2008; Farhangi, 2010; Wolsink, 2012):

- Distributed generation, mainly based on hydro, wind, and photo-voltaic energy.
- Distributed storage capacity – mainly based on batteries.
- Two-way flow of electricity and information between all nodes.
- Self-healing functionality that identifies and mitigates failures.

The "traditional" power grid does not include any of these features. Two-way communication between nodes in the grid opens up a wealth of customer services linked to sensors, power-monitoring, and automated power-transactions as part of the energy management of households.

Normally, the smart grid will offer electricity to anyone connected to the grid, just as the traditional power grid. The usage of one customer will not affect others due to the number of users connected to the grid. The smart grid appears therefore as a non-rival good. Customers may face different price models that are more or less affordable. Thus, the electricity offered through a smart grid is in this case excludable, just as electricity distributed through a traditional grid. Hence, the electricity provided in a smart grid may be a toll supply ("S4").

However, the four features of the smart grid suggest that the power plants will be less dominant market actors due to the rising number of power generators in the grid. We expect reduced rivalry among suppliers to the grid when the smart grid is further developed. Hence, this will still be a toll good in the utility-layer ("U4") after the smart grid is introduced, while the position in the supply-layer may shift:

In addition, if a *large* share of the consumers generate their own power, this will affect the option of differentiating the product through pricing models. We presume that the individual customers have significant influence over the price level of their self-generated electricity. A large share of customers consuming self-generated electricity will alter the excludability of the supply of this good. Self-generating customers will challenge the position of the large power plants. If a large share of the capital costs related to the distribution is in the hands of the self-generating electricity consumer, the cost – and ownership – of this electricity belongs to those connected to the grid. If we take into account that future exchanges and transmissions of power is taken care of by cognitive networks handling smart contracts, the marketability of electricity consumption will be further reduced (Sikorski et al., 2017). In this case we see the contours of electricity as a private good in the utility layer ("U3"), and transforming into a joint and non-excludable good fulfilling the criteria of a shared supply ("S1").

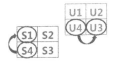

Figure 3.5 Changing positions in Figure 3.1: Smart grids substituting traditional electricity grids when customers share power generation.

Table 3.3 Four examples of changes in public goods affecting the supply-layer. (See Figure 3.1.)

Public good	Change	Public good trajectories
1 Hospital care	Growing turnover of private hospitals	U3 (S1+S2 => S3)
2 University education	Growing turnover of private universities	U4 (S2 => S3)
3 Accommodation	Airbnb challenging the hotel business	U3 (S3 => S4)
4 Electricity distribution	Smart grid substituting traditional power grids	U4 (S3 => S4)
	Advanced smart grid based on distributed generation	U4 => U3 (S4 => S1)

Summarizing the four examples

These four changes all concern excludable public goods. New technology, new organizational structures, and new policies influence the manner in which these goods are provided. In all cases, we see changes in the positions in the supply-layer, but only in one case we find that the position in the utility-layer changes. This is summarized in Table 3.3.

Notes

1 Musgrave and Musgrave (1973) made the distinction between "rivalry" and "non-rivalry" without referring to "jointness". Here we present the categories of Ostrom and Ostrom (1977), but also of Head (1962) and Buchanan (1968). The jointness-rivalry dimension captures the distinction made by Holtermann (1972) between the properties of the total amount of the good and the individual utilization of the good: "Jointness" refers to how the good is best utilized, or enjoyed by any individual, while "rivalrous" refers to a quality linked to the total amount of the good (where there are marginal costs).
2 The literature often refers to "public goods" as any good that is not strictly private. It would therefore be useful to reserve "public goods" as a reference to any non-private good. In addition, the production and consumption of private goods, with virtually no exception, produce externalities that have negative and positive effects on "the public". Thus, both private and non-private

goods have a public impact. In this text it is therefore chosen to refer to "public goods" as any kind of good with an impact on third parties.

3 Desmarais-Tremblay (2014) argues that the significance of group size is not displayed in the four public good categories and that this should therefore be included as an extension of the cells in the 2 X 2 matrix. However, this is not a refinement that other scholars have copied.

4 Ver Eecke (1999) is one that demonstrates this, based on different understandings of a public good. Most scholars distinguish between "non-rival" and "rival". However, some (e.g. Head, 1962; Olson, 1971; Ostrom & Ostrom, 1977) refer to "jointness" instead of "non-rival". This shows that this dimension covers two related issues: The degree of rivalrous good, and the degree to which the good is best appreciated by a group rather than by an individual.

5 These are often referred to as Porters' "five forces" because they also include the bargaining power of suppliers and buyers. However, this bargaining power is just as much determined by the power of the firm itself as by the suppliers and buyers and therefore not included here. Porter addresses the firm level – the rivalry firms may be subjected to – while the rivalry characterizing a public good addresses the market level – how a good behaves under different market conditions.

6 Where there is elastic demand the demand of users/consumers is sensitive to the price: E.g. the demand (and the volume of the product/service) increases when the price is reduced, and vice versa for inelastic demand.

7 This has been documented in a case study of the world's first modern lightship established in 1731 on the banks of the Thames in England (Candela & Geloso, 2018). This article makes reference to Coase (1974).

8 Several scholars have debated the status of the lighthouse services. Among these are Zandt (1993) who criticizes Coase for relying on the dichotomy of either a private or a government provided good, Bertrand (2005) arguing that the lighthouse services described in Coase (1974) fulfils the demands of the "Problem of Social Cost", described by Coase himself in 1960, and Barnett and Block (2007) who criticizes Coase (1974) for failing to point out that the companies in charge of lighthouses in the early 19th century were not a free and independent corporation of the kind we see today.

9 We find a similar and even more dismissive critique of this understanding of public goods in Hoppe (2007).

10 This is based on the individual student's perspective. If we consider education as a generic good for the society as a hole, there is a significant spill-over effect. Those who receive advanced (and useful) education benefit the society, not merely themselves. Thus, education could also be categorized as a non-excludable good.

11 Source: Figure B5.1 in the OECD publication "Education at a glance 2017". (OECD, 2017c).

12 This data is from 2015/2016 and includes USA, Japan, Australia, Korea, Italy, Poland, and Norway (*OECD, 2017a*, p. 212).

13 Source: OECD publication «State of higher education 2015–2016" (OECD, 2017d, p. 6).

14 This is in line with Marginson (2016) who claims that the public good category of university education depend on how higher education is organized. "In highly stratified systems with tuition barriers, as in the US, the private good element is strong. In more universal and less competitive Nordic-style education, most

graduates have similar standing, and the good should be classified as less rival-rous and excludable" (Marginson, 2016, p. 6).

15 This account of Airbnb is based on its business model in 2017–2018. Source: www.airbnb.com.

16 Source: An estimate published on the website kookie.cz. Retrieved from http://kookie.cz/ilovedata/2017/08/06/airbnb-growth-and-market-share/

4 The value-added process linking the utility-layer and the supply-layer

The conversion-layer

Neither the supply-layer nor the utility-layer incorporate efforts over time. These layers tell us something about the predicted utility of the good itself and the manner in which the good is provided, but they do not include any variable characterizing the work process involved in making the good providable. We may link the two layers by referring to characteristics of the value-added process from the utility-layer to the supply-layer. We refer to this layer as the "conversion-layer". This layer is conceived of as orthogonal to the supply-layer and the utility-layer (Figure 4.1), and is based on the claim that our value creation and our resource productivity relies on our ability to preserve the energy and the materials we depend on in our economy. In a wide study of extent literature and business practices Hopkinson, Zils, Hawkins, and Roper (2018) show that value-added in business may be measured by the amount of regenerated and reused energy and materials. Thus, the main performance criterion is the level of recycling and the resource productivity measured by energy units.

Determining the position of a public good in the conversion-layer

It is suggested that the position in the conversion layer is determined by two dimensions:

- The exergy[1] efficiency which refer to the amount of useful work per cost unit of the product or service (Ayres & Warr, 2009).
- The proportion of the involved substances that are recycled. How the recycling occurs depends on the substance to be recycled. It could be through material recycling, refurbishment, or re-use (Srivastava, 2007; Neto, Walther, Bloemhof, Van Nunen, & Spengler, 2010; Hopkinson et al., 2018).

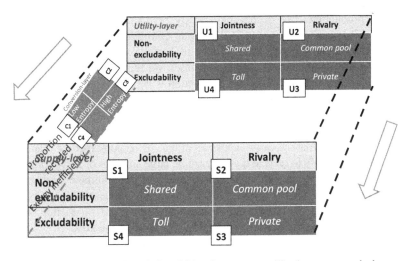

Figure 4.1 Public goods: Distinguishing between a utility-layer, a supply-layer, and a conversion-layer.

Table 4.1 Public goods: The quadrants of the conversion-layer.

	High proportion of materials recycled	Low proportion of materials recycled
High exergy efficiency	C1. **Lowentropy** (exergy efficient high recycling ratio)	C2. Exergy efficient, low recycling ratio
Low exergy efficiency	C4. Exergy-demanding high recycling ratio	C3. **High entropy** (exergy demanding low recycling ratio)

Quadrant "C1" in the conversion-layer is labelled "low entropy" and quadrant "C3" is labelled "high entropy". Exergy consumption and recycling correlates with certain interpretations of entropy. If we simplify, entropy can be understood as an irreversible trend affecting all closed environments. In a closed system of matter and energy the entropy increases with every physical action or transformation that occurs inside the system (according to the second law of thermodynamics). The structure of compounds and the different energy levels in closed systems will get ever more even and eventually completely uniform. Entropy in a closed system can never decrease. When the closed system reaches a state of internal equilibrium, its entropy is maximized. Exergy is by definition low-entropy energy which humans may utilize. Increasing exergy efficiency, everything else equal, reduces the rate of entropy production. Similarly, increasing recycling of materials avoid unnecessary extraction of natural resources and waste production. The decreasing entropy production in one subsystem happens often at the expense of increasing entropy production in another subsystem. When humans develop new technologies but at the same time emit significant amounts of greenhouse gases, we can assume there are subsystems where the rate of entropy production is declining at the expense of the entropy production in other subsystems. To the extent that we manage to reduce the rate of anthropogenic entropy production on earth, we may still increase the entropy at the scale of the solar system.

It is apparent that the two dimensions in the conversion-layer are related: It is relatively easy to recycle if you consume large amounts of exergy, and it is easy to reduce the amount of consumed exergy if you minimize the degree of recycling. In addition, a low level of recyclability indicates high impact externalities (e.g. waste/emissions) originating from the production and transport or any other work related to the provision of the good.

How does this fit with the first two layers? The position in the conversion-layer is an expression of resource efficiency related to the scarcities and vulnerabilities of the surrounding eco-system. The conversion-layer becomes a quality associated with the trajectory we see from the utility-layer to the supply-layer over time. It is the rate of entropy production, or the degree of efficiency, associated with the process of converting *potential* utility of a public good into *enabled* utility. Or, put simply, it qualifies how the good is provided to the user/consumer.

Examples of changes referring to the conversion-layer

It may be useful to look at how examples of changes to public goods influence the positions in the conversion-layer. We therefore revisit the four examples described in the previous chapter. Then we will consider carbon tax as a last example, highlighting an active involvement of the state.

Example 1: Growing private hospital sector

We see an increase in the ratio of doctors/patients, and smaller units, in private hospitals compared to in public hospitals, and it seems that private hospitals manage to put in place a more efficient utilization of material resources and of their premises by being more flexible than public institutions (Hsu, 2010; Basu, Andrews, Kishore, Panjabi, & Stuckler, 2012). A greater ratio of doctors/patients and smaller units suggests lower exergy efficiency and a more efficient utilization of material resources due to greater flexibility. This suggests an improvement of recycling and a change from a "C2" position ("Exergy efficient, low recycling ratio") to a "C4" position

("Exergy-demanding high recycling ratio") when private hospitals become more dominant.

Example 2: Growing turnover of private universities

The trend towards an increasing turnover of private universities do not seem to suggest any clear implications for changes in the position in the conversion-layer.

Example 3: Hotels losing market shares to online sharing of accommodations

The increasing market shares of online accommodation services leads to a better utilization of square meters in dwellings and, to some degree, to a substitution of hotel capacity. Exergy consumption is more effective when less exergy is wasted on empty homes. This suggest a change in the position in the conversion-layer when online sharing services win market shares from "C3" (exergy demanding/low recycling ratio) to "C1" (exergy efficient/ higher recycling ratio). Thus, in this case we see less entropy production.

Example 4: Smart grids substituting traditional power grids

When smart grids substitute traditional power grids with a distributed power generation of energy, it is expected that the share of renewable energy will increase. Thus, the rate of recycling will grow. In addition, it is expected that smart grids with monitoring devices and optimization mechanisms will lead to a more exergy efficient energy consumption. The introduction of smart grids may be interpreted as a change in the position in the conversion-layer from "C3" (exergy demanding/low recycling ratio) to "C1" (exergy efficient/high recycling ratio). Thus, this change will lead to less entropy production.

Final example: Carbon tax

The conversion-layer not only adds a quality to our understanding of how public goods are provided, it may also show the characteristic features of efforts aiming to minimize *anthropogenic shared bads*.[2] That is, non-excludable bads that humans experience together as a group.

An example of such a bad are anthropogenic carbon dioxide emissions. Many countries have introduced a carbon tax (Carbon Tax Center, 2019), and Canada is one of the first countries to introduce a "revenue-neutral" carbon tax (Rivers, 2014; The Guardian, 2018). This means that most of the revenue generated by the tax is directly returned to the taxpayers in the form of tax rebates. If we take a closer look at carbon dioxide emissions and taxation, we may distinguish between three situations:

1 No taxes related to carbon dioxide emissions.

- Emissions are negative externalities due to energy use.
- Emission characteristics as a public good:

  i A shared bad ("U1" = "S1") and is not contained in any way.

2 There is a value-added tax on carbon dioxide emissions.

- Emissions are negative externalities due to energy use.
- Emission characteristics as a public good:

  i For the public: A shared bad ("U1" = "S1").
  ii For those who pay the tax:

  - A fixed cost and they appear as a private bad ("S3").

3 There is a revenue-neutral carbon tax.

- Emissions are negative externalities due to energy use.
- Emission characteristics as a public good:

  i For the public: A shared bad ("U1" = "S1").
  ii For those who pay the tax:

  - The emissions appear as a private bad ("S3")
  - The tax rebate appears as a common pool supply ("S2") by minimizing energy use based on energy use sources that create carbon-dioxide emissions. Thus, it minimizes entropy ("C1") related to the carbon-dioxide emissions.

Regulators that implement a revenue-neutral carbon tax seems to link a *created* common pool supply ("S2") – the tax rebate – with the private incentive to minimize energy costs ("S3"). This link appears as an incentive to minimize the use of fossil energy, and thereby reducing entropy production linked to carbon dioxide emissions ("C1").

Notes

1 Exergy is in the literature defined as "the available energy for conversion from a donating source" (Hammond & Stapleton, 2001, p. 147). This is equivalent to the definition in Ayres (1998, p. 192) where exergy is defined as "the potential

work that can be extracted from a system". Exergy is normally not recycled, it is consumed or destroyed. On the other hand, energy is *always* conserved. Rosen (2005) shows that exergy prices almost always correlate with the global market prices of important commodities. It often turns out that the cost of operating a system is closely related to its exergy efficiency. The study of these variables utilizing econometric models is labelled the "Useful Work" approach by Kümmel (2011, p. 219).

2 A "bad" may be characterized as a public good with a negative impact to something treasured by humans, or anything with a negative value for the consumer or customer.

5 Descriptive and predictive value of a multi-layered approach to public goods

What do we achieve by studying public goods in a framework consisting of the three layers proposed here? First, we shall consider how these layers may be useful in accounts of the commons in ancient times. Then we will show how a multi-layered approach to public goods may be useful when we consider current issues in the social science literature.

Public goods in ancient times

The role of the commons during the Neolithic transition

The most frequently used example of a commons is a shared grazing pasture. The commons became important during the human transition from nomadic hunters and foragers to settlements of farmers during the Neolithic transition, beginning approximately 12 thousand years ago. According to Bender (1978) the introduction of agriculture may partly be explained by a *commitment* – a collective resolve. The Neolithic transition required new social relations, not only new technologies. The domestication of animals was essentially a social phenomenon that required a scaling of production that allowed the farmers to produce a surplus of food, which again requires herding (Hole, 1984). Systematic guarding of livestock animals within certain perimeters over time became essential for the economy of settlers. Human control over herds assured accessibility and the required quality. Hole (1984) suggests that this led to the development of a sense of rights linked to a delimited territory that resembles our understanding of "property" today.

The kind of property that evolved in the early phase of the Neolithic period seems to be in line with what Usher (1954) refers to as "regulated rights". This right does not correspond to the present concept of individual ownership. Regulated rights concern the rights and obligations of a group. These rights were often restricted to protect common resources. It could be to in order to ensure a sustainable felling of trees, a sustainable drainage of freshwater, or to protect newly cultivated land.

The Enclosure Movement in England, most active in 1450–1640 and 1750–1860 (Encylopædia Britannica, 1967, vol. 8, p. 361) created private ownership to land where there before was a commons. In the words of Rifkin (2014, p. 31):

> After centuries in which people belonged to the land, the land now belonged to the individual people in the form of real estate.

In the 18th century, the understanding of individual and collective ownership was no longer confined to land and herds. The understanding expanded to different kinds of intangible goods, goods based on an expected future value, and political rights (Gordon, 1995). Vandevelde (1980) characterizes this development as a "dephysicalization of property rights". The expansion of individual ownership rights seems to have happened at the expense of regulated rights of groups. According to Usher (1954), "rights of use" becomes more difficult to administer when arable land becomes scarcer in 18th-century Europe. The modern concept of private property emerges:

> The gradual disappearance of the general rights to clear new plots and to graze the animals freely in fallow and commons, and the replacement of these rights by the permanent right of each cultivator family over particular pieces of land, is only one link in the chain of events which gradually changes the agrarian structure in such a way that private property in land becomes a dominating feature.
>
> (Boserup, 1965, p. 76)

According to Hardin (1968) plots where the rights of use were regulated, referred to as "the commons", had to be abandoned as the human population increased. Today many scholars believe the commons, or natural resources provided as a common pool good, is the optimal form of governance only when the value of the good is relatively low compared to the cost of defending the good (Acheson, 2015).

In ancient times the commons was instrumental in the transition from a "direct", to a "delayed" return system when agriculture substituted hunting and foraging as the dominant way of living (Bender, 1978). But when land became scarce, and population density increased, individual ownership of land and natural resources started to substitute the regulated rights of the commons – the common pool goods. We see a trajectory in the utility layer from a common pool good ("U2"), during the early period of farming, to a private good ("U3") in the modern agricultural era. When ownership characteristics were developed the provision of the good became an exchange predicated on debt. Without a sense of otherness between two parties, a reciprocal obligation would cease to exist (Harvey, Smith, & Golightly, 2018, p. 80).

One feature distinguishing the utility-layer and the supply-layer is that the first describes the *potential* utility of goods, while the second describes *enabled* utility of goods. The position in the supply layer indicate how goods are provided or offered to users/customers. Before our societies reached an advanced level of division of work and developed well-functioning markets, there was little difference between a good's position in the utility-layer ("the good itself") and its position in the supply-layer (the good as it is provided). The trajectory "U2" => "U3" of land property in the utility-layer happens in an ancient society where the individual supplier belonged to a relatively small group. The providers of goods utilizing the commons, control a significant volume of goods relative to the supply, and is exposed to competitive pressures from other individuals. Thus, suppliers of goods utilizing the commons are exposed to rivalry in the supply-layer, and the goods originating from the commons (skin, meat, cereals etc.) are distributed according to tradition and was most likely favouring certain groups over others. Suppliers treated users/consumers within the same need category differently. Thus, the supply of goods utilizing the commons fitted the "private supply" position ("S3") in the supply-layer even before the transition from a common pool good ("U2") to a private good ("U3") in the utility-layer.

In ancient times, the proportion of recycled goods originating from a commons were most probably higher than today as a larger share of the goods were organic and soluble. It is also likely that the exergy efficiency – the amount of utility per exergy unit (unit of useful energy) – consumed was relatively low compared to today due to the lack of technology allowing humans to boost productivity expressed as the ratio of utility/exergy-consumption. Thus, in ancient times, the goods utilizing a commons qualified as "high recycling proportion" and "low exergy efficiency" in position "C4" in the conversion-layer.

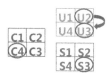

Figure 5.1 The development of the commons in the Neolithic transition. Positions in the utility-layer, conversion-layer and supply-layer as the first marketized private goods emerge.

City structures and the first public goods

Goods attained by individuals in ancient hunting and foraging communities, seem not to fulfil the criteria of *any* of the four public good categories. These goods obviously qualify as "excludable", but they hardly qualify as either "joint" or "rivalrous". Goods in ancient hunting and foraging communities originated from the residents' immediate environment, and was processed only to a limited degree. There were few incentives for exchanging goods as communities were small and relatively isolated. The goods utilized by early hunting and foraging communities may be referred to as "subsistence goods". They were excludable, but not exchangeable in a way that qualifies the good as rivalrous, and not utilized by a group in concert in a way that qualify them as a joint good. However, the emergence of organized communities with some degree of functional specialization, coincides with the emergence of public goods.

The transition from the tribal village to city structures was well under way some 5,000 years ago. By 3000 B.C. urban populations were distinguished by literacy, technology progress, social controls, political organization, and emotional focus formalized in religious-legal codes and symbolized in temples and city walls (Encyclopædia Britannica, 1967, vol. 5, p. 809). How did the formation of organized communities relate to the emergence of public goods? Most scholars agree that the formation of cities was related to the desire for goods that were only available when citizens collaborated and lived in close proximity to each other. Thus, a demand for public goods stimulated the growth of city structures;

> If citizens consume a public good that requires physical proximity for collective consumption, the concentration of consumers will cause the development of a city.
>
> (O'Sullivan, 2006, p. 41)

Work specialization was more advanced in emerging cities and created a sense of interdependence:

> even the earliest urban communities must have been held together by a sort of solidarity missing from any neolithic village. Peasants, craftsmen, priests and rulers form a community, not only by reason of identity of language and belief, but also because each performs mutually complementary functions, needed for the well-being . . . of the whole.
>
> (Childe, 1950, p. 16)

Scholars view both public goods and cities as outcomes of new technologies and competences that allowed a more stable life, and in particular, allowing residents to shorten the fallow period (the period in which the soil is left uncultivated to regain its fertility). They no longer had to change their plots of land to ensure their livelihood. This was a factor explaining why city structures evolved in ancient times, according to Boserup (1965). Hayami (2005) claims that the development of larger and more dominant cities in the 18th and 19th centuries was due in part to the ongoing shortening of the fallow period.

It is not under dispute that public goods first became a significant factor in the economy after the formation of cities and the collective surplus allowed a privileged elite to spend time on crafts, trade, security, and religious practices separated from the daily routines of the rest of the population. Many scholars point out that the development of public goods in ancient cities were related to the growing importance of infrastructures, the development of complex supply chains, the increasing surplus that allowed for a specialized workforce, and the growing collective consciousness and solidarity of the city population (Childe, 1950; Boserup, 1965; Coase, 1974; O'Sullivan, 2006.)

Public infrastructure is normally a shared good. In ancient times this could be city-walls for defence, dams for irrigation, water pipes and aqueducts for water distribution, seamarks for maritime navigation, or watchmen for ensuring security and order. These goods are not rivalrous, and they are not easily excludable. The control of these goods was in the hands of the sovereign. The provision of the goods did not change the access, or the utility, based on the inherent qualities of the good itself. The means of distribution and exclusion of economic exchange and the economic incentives did not permit the provider of infrastructures to discriminate systematically between groups of users/consumers, or create any kind of market for these infrastructure services. Thus, infrastructures in ancient cities resemble shared goods both when we consider the good itself in the utility-layer, and when we consider how the good was provided in the supply-layer ("U1" + "S1").

The development of complex supply chains is linked to the specialization of labour and the development of new technology (Childe, 1950, p. 7; Davis, 1955, pp. 430–432; Adams, 1960, p. 10). In trade, faster and more robust ships and more precise navigation was critical. This contributed to more widespread trade and a wider variety of products were offered for sale. When craftsmen and traders introduced more advanced technologies and expanded their trade network, the supply chains became more complex. Adams (1974) holds that it is important to distinguish between the "trade of goods" and the less qualified "diffusion of goods". "Trade" involves the supportive functions of the institutional structure, and strategic planning and innovation. When cities started to rely on this kind of trade, more complex supply chains were developed. At this point the need for risk mitigation and buffers arises, creating a role for common pool goods. In particular, new technology allows cities to accumulate energy-reserves. It could be firewood storages, water reservoirs, or coal deposits. In addition, several societal functions relied on a specialized competence provided by an increasingly stratified population.[1] The number of competent persons were always limited. Thus, the rivalrous good, the "competent worker", created a need for buffers to mitigate risks related to complex supply chains. It could be by hiring a surplus of workers in public work projects, or by acquiring slaves to ensure full control of the workforce. Thus, more complex supply chains created a need for common pool goods ("U2") both to increase the welfare of the community and to mitigate risks in the supply chain. The supplier of these common pool goods was normally the sovereign, and the means of providing these goods did not alter the access or utility based on the inherent qualities of the good itself. Thus, the goods acting as buffers in an increasingly complex supply chain resemble common pool goods, both in the utility-layer and in the supply-layer ("U2" + "S2").

The specialized workforce and the new technology developed in the first cities not only produced tradable goods for religious and political leaders and other privileged classes. Specialized workforces increasingly produced private goods ("U3") in exchange for work (O'Sullivan, 2006, p. 50). The pottery and cereals temple masters exchanged for work are both rivalrous and excludable. They are both rivalrous because they were acquired through a competitive exchange; the workforce could rarely choose their master, but masters competed for workers. Thus, the privileged classes offering private goods in exchange for work were rivalrous. These kinds of goods therefore resemble private supply goods ("S3"). It follows that the first private goods and private supplies depended on a surplus that required a part of the privileged class to specialize in exchange agreements, and specialized work allowing the exchange of manpower for commodities. (O'Sullivan, 2006, p. 41). This is in line with Bromley (1989), who argues that "property regimes" (distinguishing between private property, common pool property, state property, and non-property) differ with regard to the size of the surplus they require. Private property is often the most demanding, requiring a substantial surplus.[2]

The growth in the number and density of dwellings in villages transforming to cities is the foundation of growing collective consciousness and solidarity (Childe, 1950, pp. 7–16; Adams, 1960, pp. 4–7), and creates an incentive for investments in common pool goods and private goods, but also goods that are utilized collectively, toll goods. Toll goods are utilized jointly by a collective, but are at the same time excludable. Examples of toll goods in local governance are the organized worship and rituals: Temples, theatres, and sporting arenas (Childe, 1950, p. 12). Private suppliers will offer joint goods as long as they are excludable, that is, as long as they may be traded, and it is possible to gain a profit. We conclude that the public good related to a growing collective consciousness and solidarity in cities are positioned as a toll good both in the utility-layer ("U4"), and in the supply-layer ("S4"). Figure 5.2 summarizes the rise of public goods during the development of early city structures.

The emergence of public goods has much in common with the emergence of the state. The security provided by the state described in social contract theory is one of the first examples of a man-made non-excludable good. According to Fukuyama (2011, p. 82) tribal societies provided only limited public goods of this kind due to their lack of centralized authority. The four factors Fukuyama highlight as contributing to the emergence of the state seem to emulate the emergence of the public goods. The first factor is the need for a surplus to develop activities beyond the imperatives of the subsistence economy. At this point we see the emergence of infrastructures (shared goods), and the first tradable and rivalrous goods (private goods). The second factor Fukuyama highlights is the need for a certain scale of the state to allow for a minimum division of work and a ruling elite. This coincides with the need for resource buffers to mitigate the risks of complex and vulnerable supply claims. These buffers need to be managed collectively – sometimes by the use of coercion – by the ruling elite (common pool good). The third factor is the density of the population dependent on the city structure allowing the society to rely on individuals contributing to a collective good without benefiting proportionally (common pool good). The fourth factor highlighted by Fukuyama is the motivation of those contributing to the public good. Charismatic leadership could play a significant part here. We see the emergence of joint excludable goods in organized worship and other kinds of rituals (toll goods).

An alternative story of collective organization is presented by Richard Bendix (1977, pp. 59–60). When equalitarian ideas of citizens and of

Infrastructure (defence, water distribution, navigation)	**U1-S1**
Division of work created the need for buffers	**U2-S2**
First tradable rivalrous goods	**U3-S3**
Worship/Rituals	**U4-S4**

Figure 5.2 Emerging city structures and public goods. Positions in the utility-layer, and the supply-layers do not deviate.

plebiscitary democracy spread in the build-up to the French Revolution, individuals seek to enjoy their newfound freedom and independence. Bendix refers to Tocqueville's paradox; when many mutually independent men from many classes oppose aristocratic privileges, there is a tendency for the centralized power of the state to grow. To counter-act this threat men must cultivate the art of associating together. Thus, public goods must be developed within the state to limit the degree of centralization of power (e.g. the right to vote in political elections and the rule of law in the executive branch) and within the private sector (e.g. charities and gazettes) to counterbalance the state itself.

Summarizing historical examples of public goods

The land property utilized by collectives – the commons – has been gradually transformed from a common pool good to a private good when productive land became scarce and population density increased. The supply of commodities utilizing the commons fitted the "private supply" category even before the transition from a common pool good to a private good in the utility-layer. In the conversion-layer the goods utilizing the commons qualified as "high recycling proportion" *and* "low exergy efficiency". Thus, it fitted the "exergy-demanding high recycling ratio": Position "C4".

The relationship between the city structures and public goods is considered for each category of public goods:

- The development of critical infrastructure led to a more significant role of shared goods.
- The development of more complex supply chains led to a more significant role of common pool goods.
- The surplus based on increasing advantages of specialization led to a more significant role of private goods.
- The collective consciousness and solidarity resulting from the increasing geographical proximity led to a more significant role of toll goods.

But new organizational principles and technologies are not the only elements explaining the emergence of public goods. Public goods may also be associated with adaptive skills of human evolution. It may be that humans are programmed to contribute to non-excludable goods. Mercier and Sperber (2017) refer to this as the hyper-social niche of humans:

> What distinguishes humans from animals, is that we are able to cooperate not only with kin, but also with strangers; not only in here-and-now-ventures but also in the pursuit of long-term goals.
>
> (Mercier & Sperber, 2017, p. 10)

They argue that the main function of human reasoning is not to enhance individual cognition, but to produce reasons for justifying oneself and that of producing arguments to convince others. The tendency psychologists refer to as "confirmation bias" should not be understood only as a weakness in individual cognition because reasoning has vital functions at the collective level. When we collaborate in large groups, certain amounts of confirmation bias can be important to ensure social coherence and effective governance. These are traits that are critical if we are to collaborate to provide non-exclusive goods. When the provision of a good depends on the participation of "followers" in a large organizational structure, we need a reasoning at the individual level which rewards trust and favours established "truths". Mercier and Sperber (2017) argues that these hallmarks of reasoning may originate from human evolution and are re-enforced by cultural influences. Thus, human evolution may have favoured individuals' contribution to non-excludable goods, not only the selective incentives designed by group leaders, as explained by Mancur Olson (1971).

These historical accounts suggest that when public goods were introduced in ancient times, their position in the utility-layer and the supply-layer did not deviate much. Virtually all production was for immediate use and only the most meagre surpluses were traded in local fairs (Rifkin, 2014). The providers of public goods did not alter significantly the access to, or the utility of, the good based on the inherent qualities of the good itself. However, after some time, the provision of the good is changed to maximize utility, surplus, their competitive position, or long-term sustainability. This is when the position in the supply-layer starts to deviate from the position in the utility-layer. In recent history it has become common that the trajectory in the utility-layer deviates from the trajectory in the supply-layer. A multi-layered approach to public goods may shed light on ongoing trends and the political process – or on the lack of a political process. This we will consider in more detail in the subsequent paragraphs.

The debate about privatizing and deprivatizing goods

A multi-layered approach to public goods influences our discussions about privatization and deprivatization. In discussions about privatization or deprivatization, the terms "private" and "public" often lack precision. Paul Starr's article "The meaning of privatization" (1988) is typical. He refers to privatization as a direction of change without denoting a specific origin or destination: Privatization is defined as a shift of affiliation from public to private production of goods and services. By referring to positions in a multi-layered approach to public goods, we may have more precise terms to our disposal.

When a good is considered a private supply ("S3"), it is normally offered by private companies in a market. These goods are offered in a manner which allows exclusion, and it should be possible to appreciate them without having to share them, or split them, with others. Thus, with a finite amount of goods the use or consumption will often be rivalrous. In this setting, arguments in favour of *deprivatization* (changing the way the good is provided away from position S3 in the supply-layer) should be influenced by whether

1   The demand for the good is linked to a basic human need – leaving rivalry *unwanted* (favouring change "S3" => "S1"/"S4").
2   Equal access/distribution is considered critical – leaving excludability *unwanted* (favouring change "S3" => "S1"/"S2").
3   The price of the provided good is close to nil – leaving excludability difficult to accomplish (favouring change "S3" => "S1"/"S2").

To *privatize* a good (shifting its position in the supply-layer to "S3") is normally considered an option in the *absence* of the three conditions above. That is, when

1   The demand for the good is not linked to an intrinsic human need.
2   Equal access/distribution is not considered critical.
3   There is a market willing to pay for the good.

The points described cover three of the six criteria for determining the position in the supply-layer in Table 3.2. The three remaining criteria, competing for the same suppliers (SL/R/S1), threats by new entrants or substitutes (SL/R/S2), or demand restricted to a fixed quantity/quality (SL/R/U1), are related to market characteristics that affect rivalry, but do not directly affect the normative factors influencing whether a good should be offered as a private or a non-private good. Thus, the remaining criteria concern market features, while the highlighted features here concern individuals' need for accessing a good (point "1") or considerations about fair distribution (points "2" and "3").

The decision to (de)privatize a good is not only affected by factors favouring certain positions in the supply-layer, it is also affected by the potential for improving resource use. It is a well-established finding in market economics that functioning markets are able to structure and incentivize actors in ways that stimulate

*   *Efficiency*, by utilizing better the available production capacity and by stimulating innovation.
*   *Customization*, by differentiating the product and adapt to different demands and tastes.

The increased efficiency of markets is often associated with markets' self-regulating properties. Karl Polanyi (1944) claimed that once the market system is established, it must be allowed to function without outside interference. Paul A. Samuelson hailed markets' ability to self-regulate:

> A competitive system of markets and prices. . . . solves one of the most complex problems imaginable, involving thousands of unknown variables and relations.
>
> (Samuelson, 1948, p. 35)

According to Friedrich Hayek, the self-regulating nature of markets is the key characteristic explaining why markets outperform economies based on central planning:

> Economic liberalism . . . regards competition as superior not only because it is in most circumstances the most efficient method known, but even more because it is the only method by which our activities can be adjusted to each other without coercive or arbitrary intervention of authority.
>
> (Hayek, 1944, p. 38)

Milton Friedman concurs, but insists that the striking feature of the market is not only the material gains, but also the flexibility it allows with regard to utilizing and improving our full capacity:

> The great achievement of capitalism has not been the accumulation of property, it has been the opportunities it has offered to men and women to extend and develop and improve their capacities.
>
> (Friedman, 1962, p. 169)

The market driven economy not only stimulates *producers* to adapt and specialize their work in order to utilize and expand their capacities, it also stimulates the *adaptation* of products to customers' needs and tastes. According to Joseph Pine, Victor, and Boynton (1993), we see increasingly turbulent business conditions, demand fragmentation, diminishing product life cycles, and more rapidly developing technology and customer interests. In this turbulent environment mass-production of standardized products is not adequate. A system for *mass customization* is needed: Developing, producing, marketing, and delivering goods in a way that is adapted to individual demands and tastes. The dilemma of having to choose between efficient mass production and innovative niche production is no longer true in many industries. In the new business organization, highly skilled craftsmen with advanced skills and efficient communication tools are motived by a desire to create. Mass customization relates to "total process efficiency", while mass production of standardized products relates to the narrower measurement "operational efficiency" (Pine, 1993, pp. 110–111).

The economic literature supports the claim that there is a potential for increasing efficiency, innovation, and customization when we privatize the provision of an excludable good. We assume that these gains are captured when we optimize the following:

<Consumed material + energy>/<Total amounts of the good traded in the market>

We need to optimize and balance the resource use (related to the consumption of materials and exergy) and the number of potential beneficiaries (related to the total market value of the good). Thus, our measurement of entropy in the conversion-layer capture some of the gains related to privatization.

We may then consider (de-)privatization of excludable goods by considering elements from the supply-layer and the conversion-layer in three areas:

- *Negligible price:* Is the real price for accessing/enjoying the good close to nil? ("Yes" favours deprivatization and "no" favours privatization. Refers to the supply-layer.)
- *Normative grounds:* Does the good cover basic human needs and is equal access/distribution considered critical? ("Yes" favours deprivatization and "no" favours privatization. Refers to the supply-layer.)
- *Expected gains:* Is there a potential for increasing efficiency and the number of beneficiaries through innovation and customization? ("Yes" favours privatization and "no" favours de privatization. Refers to the conversion-layer.)

Let us apply these arguments in four examples: Should hospitals be privatized? Should universities be privatized? Should payment services be deprivatized? And finally, should accommodation services be deprivatized? In each of these four areas it is referred to three recently published professional texts.[3]

1) Privatize hospitals?

Privatization of the public hospitals in the United Kingdom – the NHS – has been debated many times. We consider the arguments in three published texts,[4] each discussing pros and cons of privatization of NHS.

Negligible price (real prices close to nil?)

The real prices of hospital treatment are nowhere near nil. Thus, in this area there are no barriers for privatizing hospital services.

Normative ground (basic human needs and equal access)

Supporters and opponents of privatization disagree about the outcome of privatization when it comes to whether equal treatment is threatened or not. None of the texts had any explicit reference to the basic needs of patients, and only one of the texts referred to the general importance of equal access (or words to this effect). Even though there are many in the general public who consider hospital treatment as serving a basic need and believe equal access to hospital treatment is important, these factors were only in a limited degree referred to in support of keeping NHS public. Thus, the normative grounds were not exploited by those who argued against the privatization of NHS.

Expected Gains (increasing efficiency and the number of beneficiaries)

All sources appearing in these texts referred to the current performance level of NHS as unsatisfactory. Those arguing against privatization mentioned that privatization would reduce efficiency. They claimed privatization would lead to increasing costs of administration, costs of marketing, and lack of transparency/coordination. Those in favour of privatization did not have any claims related to expected influence on efficiency. Thus, expected gains were exploited by those in favour of a public owned NHS, but not by those arguing for privatization.

We conclude that the normative grounds (basic need/equal access) was not exploited by neither the proponents or the opponents of privatization of NHS, while all sources in all three texts referred to expected gains, or added costs, depending on their view on privatization. Thus, the debate about privatization of NHS seems to be dominated by arguments referring to the conversion-layer, while arguments related to the defining traits of public goods in the supply-layer are missing.

2) Privatize universities?

Universities have many functions that require them to seek funding from several sources. It is typical to have external funding of large research projects and of executive courses for professional students. However, the core function of universities is teaching students and contributing to research.

When the dominant funding of these functions is provided by the state, the university may be referred to as "public". If the dominant funding of these functions is private we refer to the university is referred to as "private". Three published texts about the university sector in England/Australia[5] discuss the arguments in favour and against privatizing universities. We consider the arguments within the same three areas as we did for hospitals.

Negligible price (real prices close to nil?)

Despite the development of massive open online courses (MOOC) and other ways of distributing knowledge through electronic channels, the real price of higher education is by no means decreasing towards nil. This particular argument for deprivatization, or for keeping universities publicly owned, may therefore be disregarded.

NORMATIVE GROUND (BASIC HUMAN NEEDS AND EQUAL ACCESS)

The general norms linked to education as a basic need (or words to that effect) was not treated in any of the three texts. Two of the texts included statements about possible impacts of the increase in tuition fees, but no text highlighted the need for, or implications arising from, keeping to the principle of equal access. Thus, just as for hospitals, the normative grounds were not explored by any of the selected texts debating (de)privatization.

EXPECTED GAINS (INCREASING EFFICIENCY AND THE NUMBER OF BENEFICIARIES)

The main focus of all three texts was on the possible impact of privatization on the quality of teaching, the quality of research, and on the institutional and private costs of education. Thus, in these texts the expected gains/costs received most attention.

We conclude that the normative grounds (basic need/equal access) was not covered in any of the three texts, while all texts referred to expected gains, or added costs, depending on their position on privatization. This indicates that the debate about the privatization of universities, just as we saw in the debate about hospitals, is dominated by arguments referring to the conversion-layer while arguments linked to the defining traits of public goods, referring to the supply-layer, are missing.

Few economists in our age are in favour of *nationalizing* private services. The term "nationalization" does not capture the many options available in deprivatization. If we apply the multi-layered approach, we may distinguish between changes that affects the provision of a service, the access to the service, and the resources involved in both providing and accessing the service, without making institutional ownership the defining criteria. This is how we approach the possible deprivatization of payment services and accommodation services in the following paragraphs.

3) Deprivatize payment services?

The debate about future payment services in Europe have for some time been linked to the adoption of the revised payment service directive (PSD2), and how this will influence payment services. PSD2 allow bank customers to use third-party providers to operate their deposit and credit accounts. These third parties may operate in the entire EU as long as they are licensed by their home state's financial authority. The directive introduces two new actors to the financial landscape: Account Information Service Provider (AISP) and Payment Initiation Service Provider (PISP). Third party providers of financial services are expected to be active competitors in the AISP and PISP market in the coming years. Banks must allow access to diverse client-facing AISPs and PISPs, enabling them to seamlessly access bank account systems via an open interface to verify availability of funds, initiate transactions, and conduct transaction-risk analysis. The final PSD2 directive was approved in November 2015 and was fully implemented in the third quarter of 2019.

We consider three professional texts[6] that discuss how public goods may be impacted by the PSD2. As with the hospitals and universities, its distinguished between negligible price, normative grounds, and expected gains.

Negligible price (real prices close to nil?)

All the three texts argue that PSD2 is part of a transition towards a more open market for payment service where banks will be seriously challenged by non-banking institutions. Prices for basic financial services for end-users is expected to fall. It is predicted that bills will be payed seamlessly at a very low cost, using Facebook or Google. This point favours deprivatization of these financial services because prices fall to the point that the basic service is no longer marketable, and because of exclusion and profitability is difficult to achieve, it may be time to leave the position of S3 in the supply-layer in favour of a shared supply ("S1") or a common pool supply ("S2").

Normative ground (basic human needs and equal access)

None of the three texts considers the transformation of payment services as related to any basic human needs fulfilled by these services. One of the texts refer to the obligation to charge the same for account access and payment initiation from all customers. Thus, the normative grounds linked to the supply-layer are only referred to by one of the texts, and only partly, as this is linked to the properties of the future payment system – not the normative principles of the author.

Expected Gain (increasing efficiency and the number
of beneficiaries)

The main emphasis in all three texts is the expected influence of PSD2 on costs and revenues of future payment services. Non-banks will challenge the role of banks in payments services. The traditional business model of deposit banks will, according to all three texts, be economically unviable after PSD2 is fully implemented. Thus, we see changes that makes the present model of private payment services non-marketable. The PSD2 will require new business models and non-bank actors may become the dominant providers of payment services in the future.

We conclude that the impact of new technology, and the PSD2 in particular, seem to fulfil criteria in favour of deprivatization of the traditional payment services: Prices for payments services are falling, and at the same time it is expected that banks will be seriously challenged by non-bank competitors. This alone makes marketization of these services – without bundling or integrating them with other services – challenging. In addition, we see that the profitability of the traditional payment service providers is threatened by the new value chains, ecosystems, and business models that will be part of the changes in the wake of the implementation of PSD2. In concert these changes suggest two outcomes that are not mutually exclusive:

- It seems to be difficult to hold on to the basic payment service as a private supply ("S3"). The most relevant option seems be to treat these services as non-excludable and joint (the position of "S1" in the supply-layer) because they are difficult to marketize (prices near nil), and because many of the benefits depend on the access, and the data, provided by users sharing the same network.
- Alternatively, the basic payment services may be bundled or integrated with other money management services. The implementation of PSD2 then means that new business models and services will substitute the traditional ones. In this case we see a change in in the utility-layer – a transformation of the service itself. In this case PSD2 does not lead to deprivatization, but to a substitution of old services with new ones, and we have to wait for these to surface before we can determine the public good category.

4) Deprivatize accommodation services?

The market position of traditional hotels in Europe is challenged by platform-based accommodation services and the dominant platform is developed by Airbnb. According to some estimates Airbnb's share of the accommodation market in Europe was 10 percent in 2017, and is still growing fast (Koukal, 2017; Manthorpe, 2018). In response, the hotel chains are including elements used by platform services to stay attractive and accessible for a public expecting to browse, select, and complete their transactions on the net (Akbar & Tracogna, 2018; Richard & Cleveland, 2016).

We take a closer look at three professional texts,[7] two journal articles and one article from a news outlet, to consider how the market competition between the hotel chains and platform services is portrayed. The central theme in all texts is how the private good provided by the Hotel industry is affected by the growth of Airbnb.

Negligible price (real prices close to nil?)

Compared to the hotel industry the platform-based accommodation services have minimal capital expenditure and less administrative costs, and therefore can offer accommodation to a lower price than the asset-owning hotel businesses. But even if we see platforms offering beds for free (e.g. Couchsurfer.com), there is no trend towards a price, or fee, close to nil in the general accommodation market.

Normative ground (basic human needs and equal access)

None of the three texts refer to accommodation as a basic human need of human beings, or to principles of equal access to these kinds of goods. The focus of all texts were how Airbnb influences markets, challenges competitors, and attracts users.

Expected Gain (increasing efficiency and the number of beneficiaries)

All three texts referred to Airbnb as a business that profits by marketizing currently underutilized spare rooms and homes. Two of the texts mentions that Airbnb offers a more personalized and authentic experience than traditional hotels. The most cost effective in theory would be to let the platforms be as much peer-to-peer driven as possible, but mechanisms are needed to increase the platforms' brand value and competitive strengths vis-à-vis hotel chains. According to one of the texts, the platforms need to be more integrated by letting the platform owner be more visible and by investing more in owner-specific features.

Not any of the texts referred to here focus on the normative grounds for (de)privatization in the supply-layer. The main points made are linked to the efficiency of the good (the conversion-layer). This may be a bit surprising given that accommodation is a critical good for human beings. That is why the access, prices, and the size of dwellings in post-war Europe was strictly regulated until the 1980s (Scanlon, Whitehead, & Arrigoitia, 2014). But the three texts seem to agree that Airbnb leads to a more efficient use of resources by better utilizing spare rooms and homes. Thus, we see a reduction in the *relative* efficiency of traditional hotels compared to Airbnb when we focus on the means of providing accommodation. The challenge Airbnb raises for the hotel industry is that it introduces a toll supply ("S4")[8] threatening the private supply ("S3") provided by the traditional hotel industry.

Summing up

These four examples show that when we apply the multi-layered approach to public goods in discussions about (de)privatization, it allows us to distinguish between the price-, the normative-, and the efficiency-related arguments, and at the same time consider changes in the provision of goods without restricting the discussion to what sector (public or private) we believe should own, produce, or provide the good. This is all related to the multi-layered approach to public goods which allows us to distinguish between the good itself, and the provision of the good. We may illustrate the four examples with reference to the three public good layers ("U" = utility, "C" = conversion, and "S" = supply) (see Figure. 5.3).

When a (de)privatization process does not involve a radical innovation changing the characteristics of the good itself, but is more about changing the provision of the good (as shown in Figure 5.4 for hospitals and universities), the debate seems to focus on efficiency implications linked to alternative provisions, not on how to provide the good – rivalrous or joint access? – excludable or not? When the (de)privatization process *does* involve a radical innovation that changes the characteristics of the good itself (as shown in Figure 5.4 for payment services and accommodation services), the debate seems to focus on efficiency implications, as in the first two examples, but the question of how the good should be provided is then missed because the "old" and the "new" should be considered as two separate goods.

When the implications of different kinds of provisions of public goods are omitted in the debates about (de)privatization, we are left with considering the implications for efficiency – the sustainable costs and gains related to the conversion-layer and the number of beneficiaries. But the

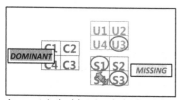

Arguments in the debate on whether hospitals should be privatized.

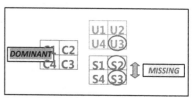

Arguments in the debate on whether universities should be privatized.

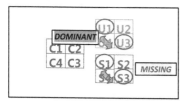

Arguments in the debate on whether payment services should be deprivatized.

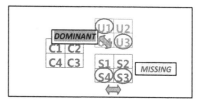

Arguments in the debate on whether accommodation services should be deprivatized.

Figure 5.3 Public good references in the professional texts.

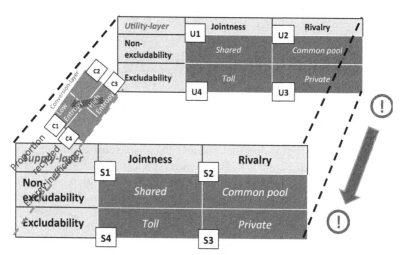

Figure 5.4 Radical innovations referring to properties of the public good. Assumed radical innovations contribute to changes in the positions and directions highlighted.

efficiencies and number of beneficiaries are to a great extent influenced by how we choose to provide the good. The missing arguments on the normative grounds related to the type of public goods, may be because this is considered a given: Once the technology and the good itself is defined and made available, the question of choice of provision is thought of as *politics*, or as an unwarranted *intervention* in the value chain of technologies and calculated efficiencies. The lack of a fully fledged debate on the implications of changing public goods may then be due to the limited focus of different academic subject areas: Political scientists are typically drawn to normative questions related to institutional powers and distribution, while economists have a preference for quantitative problem solving linked to a set of explicit assumptions.

It is worth mentioning that the debate on public goods may involve a fourth topic, in addition to the price, the normative grounds and the efficiency. We may question whether it is right, no matter how we ensure proper access and quality, to marketize the good. Radin (1987) states that certain things should neither be considered as a commodity (not suited for marketization) nor as a non-tradable good. There is a third category, according to Radin: Things that are *market-inalienable*. Radin refers to three examples of market inalienables; prostitution, baby-selling, or surrogate motherhood. Similar arguments are presented in Blomqvist (2004) and Svanborg and Sjövall (2014) against the privatization of care services and other services where quantitative performance variables are considered unfit. We shall now leave the debate on (de)privatization and turn to how this approach to public goods may influence our understanding of innovation.

Qualifying innovations

Since the publication of "Business Cycles" by Joseph A. Schumpeter in 1939, it has been commonly accepted that innovations are not limited to technical inventions, production methods, and new commodities. The opening of new markets, the discovery of new sources of supply, and new and more effective ways of organizing and governing businesses are significant kinds of innovations as well. Schumpeter argued that innovation is the most important factor explaining growth in market economies even though it is difficult to incorporate in general equilibrium models. The growth of the economy is due to changing factors in the production function resulting in a higher output (more employees, more resources, larger machines etc.), but it was also due to transformations of the production function itself, according to Schumpeter.

The fundamental impulse that sets and keeps the capitalist engine in motion comes from the new consumers' goods, the new methods of production or transportation, the new markets, the new forms of industrial organization that capitalist enterprise creates.

(Schumpeter, 1942, pp. 82–83)

Anything causing significant changes to the production function may be characterized as an innovation, according to Schumpeter. Traditionally, most of the growth in the economy was attributed to decreasing factor costs. Schumpeter argued that innovations should be a core point of the growth model:

what dominates the picture of capitalistic life and is more than anything else responsible for our impression of a prevalence of decreasing cost, causing disequilibria, cutthroat competition and so on, is innovation, the intrusion into the system of new production functions which incessantly shift existing cost curves. . . . The impression that firms moving in intervals of decreasing costs are often in the center of the vicissitudes of industrial life is not wrong. But this links up with innovation.

(Schumpeter, 1939, p. 88)

The significance of innovation for economic growth was re-emphasized in 1942:

Economists are at long last emerging from the stage in which price competition was all they saw. . . . But in capitalist reality . . . it is not that kind of competition which counts but the competition from the new commodity, the new technology, the new source of supply, the new type of organization – competition which commands a decisive cost or quality advantage and which strikes not at the margins of the profits and the outputs of the existing firms but at their foundations and their very lives.

(Schumpeter, 1942, p. 84)

The innovations Schumpeter refers to include changes to the good itself, to the processes linked to the production of the good, including how the good is provided, how it stimulates demand, and how it may create a new demand. The time-dimension is essential here. In a literature review of the innovation concept, Simula (2007) claims that commercial success is a defining trait of business innovations. Thus, innovations can only be determined retrospectively which means we need to consider the diffusion and the adoption of the good before we judge innovations.

The classic account of innovation concern topics included in each of the three public good layers: The utility-layer (the good itself), the conversion-layer (efficiency), and the supply-layer (provision). Given that the aim of the multi-layered approach to public goods is to improve our understanding of changes within these layers, and how positions in these layers are related, we should explore how the multi-layered approach may be useful when we consider innovations. We start by considering how innovation is currently measured.

Literature reviews (e.g. Smith, 2005; Adams, Bessant, & Phelps, 2006; Katila, 2007) show that innovation is measured in many different ways in academic contributions:

- By comparing numbers of patent applications. A patent is a contract, and a patent application indicates there is a belief that a particular innovation promises a return in the future. Citation-weighted patents has been shown to be a valid measure of radical innovations (Katila, 2007, pp. 308–309).
- By comparing businesses' R&D portfolio, expenditures, and personnel resources. This is related to an expectation that investments in R&D activities will pay off.
- By comparing the number of relevant scientific publications is an indicator of innovation (bibliometric data). This measurement is based on the assumption that there is a correlation between the number of such publications and innovation.
- By questioning people participating in, or observing, an innovation process. Intuitively we would assume that the number, and the degree, of changes in the public good layers corresponds to the radicalness of innovations. Based on the given characteristics of these layers, we may postulate that radical innovations are identified among two kinds of changes.

When the category of the good changes and we see a shift in the position in the utility-layer *and* the supply-layer, this is considered more radical than a change where we only see a shift in one of the layers. A shift in the supply-layer indicates a change prompted by some kind of an institutional change, or a process, while a shift in the utility-layer is due to an entire new product or service suggesting a possible new market. Following Henderson and Clark (1990) we may then differentiate between incremental, modular, architectural, and radical innovations. We may also distinguish between four kinds of radical innovations; those disruptive to industry, organizations, users, and technologies (Katila, 2007).

A change between the categories "C3" and "C1" is the most radical shift in the conversion-layer. This involves the material use and exergy consumption linked to the production of the good, and the logistics involved in providing the good. There are many studies that focus on the efficiencies in firms' innovation processes (e.g. Adams et al., 2006, pp. 36–37).

An example of a radical innovation is the introduction of the first popular crypto-currency, Bitcoin (Wörner, Von Bomhard, Schreier, & Bilgeri, 2016). Crypto-currencies are part of a peer-to-peer payment system and they are typically based on blockchain technology. They substitute traditional payment systems which depend on third-party validation and clearing. We see that Bitcoin started a transition from a private good towards a shared good ("U3"=>"U1") and from a private supply towards a shared supply ("S3"=>"S1"). The question here is if this reference to changes in the public good layers is a better indicator of radical innovations than the measures described (and criticized) by Smith (2005), Adams et al. (2006), and Katila (2007). For some purposes this is likely. The proxies used in the measurements referred to earlier lack a reference to the number of likely beneficiaries and the impact of externalities. By focusing on changes in the position in the public good layers we highlight the provision of the good and the access to the good.

The understanding of radical innovations is based on changes in the three public good layers. We determine the degree of radicalness of an innovation by distinguishing between how the innovation has changed the good itself, the provision of public good, and the resources required to enable the provision of the good. In addition, we assume that rivalrousness stimulates innovation.

Competitiveness and prices

The multi-layered approach to public goods may be a useful reference for categorizing what we believe to be competitive goods. For a good to qualify as competitive in a market, it must fulfil the following criteria:

- It must qualify as a private good or toll good in the utility-layer. Thus, the properties of the product must allow us to restrict the beneficiaries of the product to a selected group. It should be excludable.
- The manner in which the product is provided must also qualify as a private supply or toll supply. Thus, it must be practically feasible to provide the good to customers in a way that systematically favours certain sub-groups and to generate a profit.

But these criteria only tell us that competitive products must be marketable which is obvious. But the multi-layered approach to public goods may be used not only to qualify goods that may be competitive in a market, but also to consider the *degree of competitiveness* of goods: The position in the supply-layer is the result of an intended business strategy in order to realize maximum utility based on the potential utility of the good itself. However, it is the user/consumer who ultimately defines the utility of the good, influenced by marketing and branding strategies. If we assume the demand of the good as given, the task of the business is to select the following:

- The optimal good (the business model, technology, and material related to the good itself) in the utility-layer.
- The optimal manner of provision (logistics/marketing/follow-up) in the supply-layer.
- The optimal production and distribution with regard to the most efficient use of materials and exergy in the conversion-layer.

All of this is in order to generate a demand in the intended market. This is illustrated in Figure 5.5.

The multi-level approach to public goods may be applied when we consider the competitiveness of taxi services. Given the existence of the following:

- Agreed indicators showing which taxi service the users appreciate the most.
- A specified list of what contributes to increasing entropy the most, e.g. indicators of the degree of recycled elements, emissions to air, and consumption of exergy per kilometre transport.

Given these, we would expect that the most competitive taxi services would be the service that maximizes the ratio

Perceived utility/Entropy

where the "perceived utility" is the users'/consumers' perception of the enabled utility.

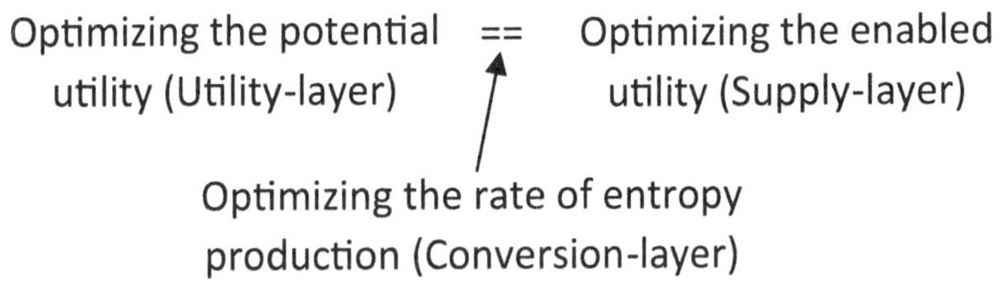

Optimizing the potential   ==   Optimizing the enabled
utility (Utility-layer)   utility (Supply-layer)

Optimizing the rate of entropy
production (Conversion-layer)

Figure 5.5 Competitiveness: Optimizing the enable utility and the level of entropy.

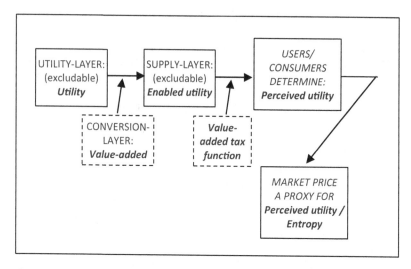

Figure 5.6 Market price based on different kinds of utilities and value-added tax.

We expect firms to minimize factors that contribute to increasing entropy by minimizing negative externalities (increasing recycling and exergy efficiency, see Figure 5.6). According to Bardy and Massaro (2013) this amounts to a shift of costs-bearers of public goods from the society (the tax-payers) to private businesses. The value-added concept is expanded to internalize firms' key externalities in line with the shared value concept (see Porter & Kramer, 2011; Laudal, 2018). Thus, we should not only focus on maximizing recycling and exergy efficiency of single firms, but also of the firms' supply chains and partnerships.

If firms pay for the "societal costs" of goods, both the committed and future costs of their own, and the most significant short- and long-term externality costs, then the market price would act as a proxy for the *<perceived utility/entropy>* (see Figure 5.6).

We shall consider what this means for our understanding of market prices. In most of the economic literature, the market price acts as a proxy for the demand relative to the supply, or, according to most economists, the market price is an *expression* of the demand and the vehicle that allows an equilibrium – a balance between the supply and demand – in the market. If we manage to design market mechanisms and a tax system that incorporate the prices of the significant negative externalities, the market price may in addition act as a proxy for the following:

• Costs related to preserving scarce resources.[9]

- Third-party costs for those that are not party of the transaction.
- Costs to the natural environment which humans depend on or value.

A fundamental freedom in liberal market economies is the firms' freedom to set its own prices within the boundaries of the law. The inclusion of costs of negative externalities should therefore be a value-added tax (VAT) designed as a function based on the price set by the firm and target three elements:

- Costs of protecting rare materials: In this area the tax function is adapted to protect the depletion of the remaining deposits of material that are considered critical to our economy.
- Third-party costs: The tax function should be adapted to cover the costs of third parties affected by the value-added of the firm.
- Natural environment costs: This tax function should be based on fixed categories/standards triggering different tax levels, not individual calculations because this is too complicated to put in place.

This means that the VAT should not be a flat tax, but adjusted to cover the significant negative externalities of individual firms, or of individual classes of firms. This new VAT should be tailored to the level of externality costs the same way trade tariffs are tailored to cover the needs of individual commodities and industries within the nation-state.

If these three VAT elements are revenue-neutral, the tax volume may be scaled to fulfil the exact financial purpose of the tax. This is in line with two key aims of the market. Prices will take into account the costs of the significant negative externalities, not only the committed and future costs of the firm. And more fundamentally, prices will be a proxy for something more than the current demand. With these three elements covered, the VAT will also be a proxy for the costs related to scarce natural resources, for third party costs, and for costs associated with the degradation of the natural environment.

Attributes of liberal democracy and political standards

The virtues of liberal democracy may be expressed by referring to the multi-layered approach to public goods. The increasing power and legitimacy of European states during the last 200 years is inseparable from the emergence of the rule of law, according to Francis Fukuyama (2011). It is evident that the "rule of law" fulfils the characteristics of a shared good ("U1"). According to Fukuyama (2011), the rule of law only exists where the law-making body is sovereign, and when also individuals holding political power are bound by the rule of law. Before we consider this further, it is worth noting that classical accounts of democracy[10] refer to different core characteristics of democracy:

- The quality of engaging with others in ways that contributes to a collective identity, and the aim of sorting out differences according to an agreed procedure to reach a consensus.
- A formal constitutional approach and a participatory discourse approach.
- Governance by townhall meetings and referendums, and governance by representatives deciding within their given mandate.

Though different scholars on democracy differ on these elements (and others), they all agree that the democracy demands a "rule of law" and that whatever the instruments and contexts we deal with, the aim of democracy should be to institute a system whereby the ultimate sovereignty emerges from the people, as put forward by J. J. Rousseau in 1791. But history shows that neither the fulfilment of the diffuse aim of supporting the "general will", nor technical rules of voting-procedures and governance, is sufficient to protect liberal democracies.[11]

One of the prerequisites of a well-functioning democracy mentioned in recent studies is a minimum level of homogeneity when it comes to both cultural attributes and household income.[12] Mukand and Rodrik (2017) refer to a formal utility model to analyze the prerequisites of a liberal democracy. They find that a liberal democracy demands mild levels of income inequality and weak identity cleavages. Mukand and Rodrik then postulate that a well-functioning liberal democracy protects the following:

- Property rights of asset holders and investors.
- Political rights and free and fair electoral contests.
- Civil rights by ensuring equality before the law and non-discrimination in the provision of public goods.

Relative homogeneity is correlated with popular support for these three universal rights. Given that the homogeneity demand is fulfilled, liberal democracy has important characteristics at two levels. At the *national governance level*, we consider the property rights, political rights, and civil rights. If they all are universal, we conclude that the rights protected at the national level in liberal democracies corresponds to a shared supply ("S1"): When a state guarantees all citizens within its borders certain rights, these rights must be characterized as a non-excludable and a joint (non-rivalrous) good. At the *service level*, an aim of liberal democracies, according to Mukand and Rodrik (2017), is to ensure non-discriminatory provision of public goods.[13] That is, liberal democracy demands a non-discriminatory provision of those goods that the state offer as "public services". "Non-discriminatory goods" may be referred to as a "non-excludable good", but does not necessarily imply a non-rivalrous good. Thus, when the state in a liberal democracy provides "public services" we would expect it to be services in the format of a shared supply ("S1") or a common pool supply ("S2").

Liberal democracy may then be characterized as a system where the *state* is responsible for basic shared goods ("U1") and provide public services fulfilling the characteristics of a shared supply ("S1"), or a common pool supply ("S2").

What role should the state not take on? Are their limitations? Referring to the multi-layered approach, the state in a liberal democracy should normally not be providing private goods ("S3") or toll goods ("S4"). The grounds for such a principle are that the state should not provide excludable goods, or goods that favour certain sub-groups within similar need categories, or goods that are marketable, because these goods are best provided by private actors in a market motivated by profit and restricted by the market demand. Excludable goods are provided more efficiently by market actors.

However, the purpose of some state services is to fill a *void* left by the market actors. Thus, states are not only needed to provide universal services, there are excludable services of critical importance to the population that have little or no chance of being launched by market actors due to the need of a substantial investment, or a major institutional capacity. This is the case for many examples of toll supply ("S4"). It could be centrally generated electricity through a national grid, public passenger transport, or toll roads.

These principles concern what kind of public goods the state is responsible for, and are referring to public good categories which could be *changed* by political divisions, affecting the goods' position in the supply-layer. The motive for such a policy decision could be a void left by the market, or any kinds of considerations convincing voters and their representations to change the properties of a public good.

There are important public goods also in the international arena.[14] Many of these goods appear as de facto political standards. It could be international treaties, harmonized national regulations and fees, and national policies. They appear as standards as they gather support from a majority of governments or market actors. Examples of such standards are the Kyoto treaty, the decisions to ban all CSC to protect the ozone layer in our atmosphere, and the decision to require all vehicles to be equipped with catalytic converters. Barrett (2002) shows that in all these cases there are standards fulfilling the characteristics of a public good. This public good is supported by contexts that include two characteristics:

1   There should be economies of scale: The marginal cost of the good should be lower than the average cost. The price for fulfilling the political standard is approaching nil. Thus, the good is non-excludable ("S1" or "S2").
2   The network of providers and users/consumers should be widespread and dense to enhance the proliferation of a political standard. And the product is not adapted to any subgroup of the potential customers. Thus, the good is non-excludable ("S1" or "S2").

This is in line with the criteria for positioning goods in the supply-layers. We see that the layers are useful to cover the government's efforts to raise these kinds of political standards.

Growth indicators

Up until now the "multi-layered approach to public goods" is presented as a vehicle that allows us to introduce more nuanced categories of public goods. These categories are useful references when changes in public goods are debated. But models in social science may also help us consider whether a specific development is *beneficial* or not, given certain criteria. More ambitious models help us to *predict* outcomes based on some specific input. It could concern questions like these: What kind of business innovations should the state support? How should the government regulate business activity that deplete precious resources or that produce harmful externalities? Or how should a particular good be provided to maximize benefits for users/consumers?

An approach to the question of optimal regulation of business, and an optimal provision of goods, is to identify:

*   *The most promising innovations.* The impact of innovations for users/consumers is considered based on market surveys of the selected groups of users'/consumers' demand.
*   *How firms should minimize the entropy related to their activities.* This can be done by considering how firms should maximize their exergy efficiency and maximize the proportion of recycled materials without reducing their product quality or harming innovation.
*   *How to maximize the user/consumer benefit.* Benefits are typically measured by the realized demand, or by the aggregate revenue in an industry.

It is difficult to measure both what determines the most promising innovation and what maximizes the user/consumer benefit of a given good. Technical variables are related to the good itself and contextual variables are related to the supply and distribution of the good.

By referring to the multi-layered approach to public goods we may highlight characteristics that indicate whether it is a radical/incremental innovation, whether it generates low/high entropy, and whether it allows access to reach a broad or narrow group of users/consumers.

Electronic services may illustrate this.[15] The proposition to assess the innovation and the number of beneficiaries of electronic services rests on two assumptions. The first assumption is that *radical innovations*, understood as changes in line with the characteristics described in the section "Qualifying innovations" above (a shift in both the utility-layer and the supply-layer), is a dummy-variable for identifying radical service innovations. The second assumption is that a change that shifts the category of a public good towards non-excludable supply (from "S3" or "S4" towards "S1" or "S2"), without reducing the quality of this good, indicates an increase in the potential number of persons benefitting from the good.[16] The quality is assured even when production is scaled up because the customization of electronic services may also be scaled up.[17] Adapting to customer-tastes is possible without systematically favouring certain groups because the good can be offered in many variants through a common access point available to all. Electronic services are not subject to subtractability and excludability to the same degree as physical goods (Harvey et al., 2018).

Producing electronic services with minimum entropy means that no energy is wasted, and that the materials are utilized to the fullest. All

---

Growth indicators of electronic services

- Indicators of a *radical innovation.*
  - o Will the innovation lead to a change in more than one layer?
- Indicators of *efficiency gains.*
  - o Will the innovation lead to a more exergy efficient service than the service it replaces or complements?
  - o Will the innovation improve the proportion of recycled materials in sourcing, production and in use/consumption of the good?
- Indicator of *a growing number of beneficiaries.*
  - o If the likelihood of exclusion is reduced by the way the service is provided. If we see a shift towards "S1" or "S2", we assume that the potential benefit of the service has increased.

Figure 5.7 Indicators of growth of electronic services.

else equal, this promises a more competitive business because resource costs and monetary costs are minimized.

Thus, if we wish to stimulate growth through the innovation of electronic services, one should stimulate radical innovations (innovations that change the category of a good in both the utility layer and supply layer), stimulate firms with the most efficient use of energy and materials (low entropy), and firms that are best at expanding their non-excludable supply (moving towards "S1" or "S2" in the supply-layer). This is summarized in Figure 5.7.

Notes

1 The population of ancient cities consisted typically of slaves, laborers, many kinds of craftsmen, merchants, landowners, governing elites, priests, and nobility. (Childe, 1950, p. 11)
2 Bromley (1989) questions the conventional economic maxim claiming that private property and related incentives explain the growing economic surplus in societies. It could be the other way around: The surplus provided by a particular natural resource or activity may determine the property regime.
3 The selection of these professional texts is based on three criteria: They should be recently published, address the stated issue, and they should be of high professional quality, published by scientific journal or in a widely respected outlet.
4 Three professional recent texts discussing the pros and cons of privatization NHS were selected. 1) *The big debate: We need to privatise NHS.* Published by two students with opposite views in the weekly student newspaper at University of Sussex; "The Badge", published March 1, 2017. 2) *The pros and cons of privatizing the NHS,* published in "The Week" April 26, 2018. 3) *Debating the future of the NHS: Hawking versus Hunt,* published in journal *BMJ* (formerly *British Medical Journal*), reporting on the debate between scientist Stephen Hawking and England's health secretary Jeremy Hunt.
5 Three professional recent texts discussing the pros and cons of privatization of universities in a western country were selected: 1) *Book review: Privatising the Public University: The Case of Law* by Margaret Thornton. *Contemporary Sociology: A Journal of Reviews* (2014) 43:581. 2) *Have England's universities been privatised by stealth?* Published in *The Guardian* (UK), October 12, 2014. 3) *What's wrong with privatising universities?* Commentary published in the national magazine of Friends of the earth in Australia; "Chain Reaction", in November 2015.
6 Three professional recent texts discussing the transformation of payment services were selected. 1) *Global Payments 2020: Transformation and Convergence,* a report published by BNY Mellon (a corporate brand of The Bank of New York Mellon Corporation), Moorgate and CPUS, in September 2014. 2) *PSD2 – the directive that will change banking as we know it.* Article published by the Scandinavian computer software and consultancy company EVRY, in 2017. 3) *PSD2: Taking advantage of open-banking disruption.* An article published on the website of the consultancy group McKinsley, in January 2018.
7 The three professional texts referred to here are about how Airbnb (platform businesses) challenge the traditional hotel business. The sample consists of

two journal articles: Richard and Cleveland (2016) and Akbar and Tracogna (2018) and one newspaper article: *Airbnb and the Unintended Consequences of Disruption'* (*The Atlantic*, Boston – US).

8 The claim that Airbnb may be categorized as a toll good is discussed earlier and is based on the assumption that Airbnb is a less rivalrous than hotel accommodation because the provision does not resemble a zero-sum game and because you need hundreds of thousands of users in order to establish an effective service.

9 Colm (1956) is one of the scholars specializing on public goods who highlights resources that are irreplaceable, or which require a long period of time for replacement. The typical argument is that without market interventions, the deposits of these resources are threatened.

10 E.g. Toucqueville (1848), Mill (1861), Schumpeter (1942), Pateman (1970), Lively (1975), and Habermas (1976).

11 This is also true when we refer to the need of incentivizing voters by referring to individual costs of voting and adding the collective gains by assuring a liberal democracy. In the calculations of Anthony Downs it does not add up, according to Dougherty (2003, pp. 247–248).

12 Some of the literature looking into this refer to "identity politics" as the policies disrupting traditional systems of democratic governance.

13 Some authors claim that the core features of the capitalistic system excludes workers from the enclosures, or from the "commonstock", of nature, of politics, and of the economy, implying that only the capital owners have full access to the rights and opportunities offered in liberal democracies and in liberal market economies (e.g. Lindblom, 1977; Anton, 2000).

14 One example of this is found in Eden and Hampson (1997). They consider how market failures and governance failures give rise to international regimes and point to four failures related to public goods: Efficiency failures, macroeconomic instabilities, distributional conflicts, and security concerns.

15 "Electronic services" is here defined as all kinds of services mediated by digitalized information and communication technology (ICT), in line with Rowley (2006).

16 For many goods a change of the category of the good towards a non-excludable good is not an option (e.g. university education). For other goods it could be claimed that the incentives for taking care of the good requires private ownership (e.g. freehold homes and cars).

17 This is referred to as "mass customization" (see Gilmore & Pine II, 1997; Unruh, 2018).

6 Public good trends

Common pool supply in decline?

Differences in purchasing power

According to Eurostat,[1] the Gini coefficients referring to disposable income in Sweden and Denmark grew from just above 26 in 2012 to nearly 28 in 2017, while the Gini coefficient of Norway grew from 22.5 in 2012 to 25 in 2017. Increasing differences in household income represent a pressure towards allowing suppliers to offer excludable goods. In particular it creates a pressure towards privatizing common pool supply ("S2").

What is the basis for this claim? A common pool supply is to be shared by a group. If the differences in purchasing power increases (everything else equal), there will be a pressure from the most affluent to be allowed to receive goods/services that only they can afford. Thus, there is a pressure to make goods excludable by changing the provision from a common pool supply to a private supply, as illustrated in Figure 6.1.

An example of this is already mentioned in the hospital sector: In many OECD economies where there is a substantial portion of affluent households, we see a 120 percent real growth of out-of-pocket insurance and employer-based insurance schemes for hospital care between 2000 and 2015 (OECD, 2017a). This leads to a pressure to transform a common pool supply ("S2") – public hospitals – to a private supply ("S3") – private hospitals.

The multi-layered approach to public goods may also help us to understand the political *in-action* when "U3" goods change their manner of provision from a common pool supply ("S2") to a private supply ("S3"). It will always be in the interest of private households to purchase the highest quality products they can afford. The differences in purchasing power among households legitimates the transformation of a common pool supply ("S2") to a private supply ("S3") because this is required if the affluent are to be offered the optimal good for them.

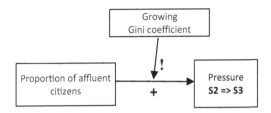

Figure 6.1 Differences in purchasing power (increasing Gini coefficients) and changes in the position in the supply-layer.

The elimination of scarcity of certain natural resources and services

When we categorize the good itself as a common pool good ("U2") the total amount of available resources is limited. The categorization may be based on a finite reservoir in nature or on the limited supply of qualified professionals. Such goods are extracted, produced, or provided in a manner which takes the limited pool of resources into account. The categorization of a common pool good does not demand any particular kind of distribution, but it typically includes a system to structure and regulate the access to the limited resource with some kind of central co-ordination.

If the implementation of new technology allows us to reduce or eliminate the scarcity of natural resources and services, the relative amount of provided common pool supply ("S2") will likely decrease. This should not affect the categories we see in the utility-layer (a wild-fish catch will always be a common pool good), but the supply-layer categories will change when new technology changes our manner of providing goods (e.g. Kindle books), and leads to the invention of new kinds of goods in the utility-layer (e.g. farmed fish).

Thus, everything else equal, we foresee a decrease in the relative amount of common pool supply ("S2") as differences in purchasing power increase, and as long as new technology contributes to the elimination of scarcity of natural resources and services.

Shared supply on the rise?

Kaul (2010) argues that the global integration of markets, government regulations, and civil society would not have been possible without a corresponding globalization of public goods. Examples are universalized human rights, the global spread of policy conditions fostering privatization and economic liberalization, and the physical infrastructures facilitating cross-border connectivity. The connectivity is related to the performance of ICT and of energy networks. Hardware, software and information download is gradually getting cheaper, and the consumption of electricity per capita is growing world-wide suggesting that the unit costs of electricity is decreasing. Rifkin (2014) refers to this, as the trend towards "The Near Zero Marginal Cost society". The International Telecommunication Union (ITU) reported in 2017 that 70 percent of all youth (between 15 and 24 years) in the least developed countries are using the internet. The percentage of the world's households having access to the internet at home increased from 30 percent in 2010 to 52 percent in 2016. In these years the world's average subscription costs of mobile broadband devices dropped by more than 50 percent. And mobile broadband connectivity is now more important than fixed broadband.[2]

In the OECD area the generation of electricity has doubled the last 40 years.[3] The consumption of electricity in EU (28) increased 31 percent between 2000 and 2015.[4] Electricity is moving from being a utility to a commodity.[5] Traditionally, electricity is distributed from large power plants through a one-directional grid to the end customers. We now see a trend towards a decentralized commodity distributed through bi-directional "smart grids" between professional generators, and from customers with spare capacity after generating electricity from their own solar cells or wind turbines. The cost of a solar array fell by around 80 percent from 2005 to 2014, and wind power remains cheaper than solar.[6]

The trends towards ubiquitous access to information and services on the Internet, are well documented by scholars (e.g. Weiser, 1991; Trivedi & Sagar, 2010; Saraswat, Gupta, & Dutta, 2018; Silva, Khan, & Han, 2018). This is also the case for the increasing consumption of electricity in bi-directional smart grids with decentralized power generation (Alstone, Gershenson, & Kammen, 2015; Kakran & Chanana, 2018). These trends transform the provision of common pool goods (e.g. traditional public mail systems), private goods (e.g. credit card payment services), and toll goods (e.g. traditional electricity grid), to shared goods (e.g. Gmail/Yahoo! mail, P2P payment services, and smart grids).

A good turns non-excludable and non-rivalrous when the following four criteria are met:

- All have access to the good.
- All can afford the good.
- The resource the good depends on are not scarce.
- The processing and consumption of the good does not produce major negative externalities.[7]

The long-term trends related to the globalization of human rights, liberal state policies, and physical infrastructures, including access to information, and trends related to the distribution and exchange of electricity, leads to the fulfilment of these criteria. Thus, this is an example of a long-term shift towards shared supply ("S1").

Notes

1 Source: Eurostat, *Gini coefficient of equalized disposable income – EU-SILC survey,* last updated October 23, 2018. Retrieved November 2018, from https://is.gd/Hy9Pye.
2 Two sources support this claim: 1) The publication, "ICT Facts and Figures 2017", published by the ITU in July 2017. Retrieved November 2018, from www.itu.int/en/ITU-D/Statistics/Documents/facts/ICTFactsFigures2017.pdf. 2) The publication "The Little Data Book on Information and Communication Technology", published by ITU in 2018. Retrieved November 2018, from www.itu.int/en/ITU-D/Statistics/Documents/publications/ldb/LDB_ICT_2018.pdf
3 Source: The publication "Electricity Information Overview", published by the International Energy Agency in 2018. Retrieved November 2018, from https://webstore.iea.org/download/direct/2261?filename=electricity_information_%202018_overview.pdf
4 Source: The publication "Energy consumption and energy efficiency trends in the EU-28 2000–2015" (page 69). Published by the European Commission in 2018. Retrieved November 2018, from http://publications.jrc.ec.europa.eu/repository/bitstream/JRC110326/efficiency_trends_2017__final_lr.pdf
5 Source: Published by the business website raconteur.net in April 2018. Entitled; "As society changes, so does the grid that powers it". Retrieved November 2018, from www.raconteur.net/technology/society-changes-grid-powers
6 Source: Text entitled "5 megatrends" for a global energy transition». Author; Craig Morris, leader of German Energy Transition. Published in July 2015. Retrieved November 2018, from https://energytransition.org/2015/07/5-megatrends-for-a-global-energy-transition/, and also the report "The digital energy system 4.0", published by ETP Smart Grids, (Vingerhoets et al.) in 2016, funded by the EU's 7th Programme for research.
7 The issue of how externalities affects the public good is not treated here. See Ayres (2016, p. 374) for the role of externalities in main stream economic research, and Laudal (2018) for a discussion on how externalities affect international business.

7 A multi-layered approach to public goods

Most of the economic literature on public goods focus on the optimal distribution and expenditure, and on problems related to collective governance. Several scholars are critical to the notion that we can govern public goods by referring only to properties of the good itself (e.g. Cowen, 1985; Stretton & Orchard, 1994; Malkin & Wildavsky, 1991). However, none of these critiques include a model which incorporates relevant institutional frameworks though these scholars take the position that institutional and political contexts *should* be recognized.

The aim of the multi-layered approach is to improve our understanding of public goods. Referring to these goods as categories determined by three layers seems to be useful. The *utility-layer* characterizes the potential utility, or the ideal utility of a good, while the *supply-layer* characterizes the enabled utility determined by the provision of the good which again is linked to institutional elements and policies, and the *conversion-layer* indicates the degree of efficiency in the use of energy and materials.

In the multi-level approach to public goods the question of whether a good may be characterized as rivalrous or excludable is determined by the good itself, but also by the institutional and political environment deciding how the good is provided. We may consider studies of how innovations contribute to economic growth. It is claimed that innovations produce a greater *social* return than *private* return. This is due to free-riders' access to the results of the innovation. However, the social return really depends on how the product/service is provided, and, in particular, how knowhow resulting from the innovation is provided to third parties.

We link the two layers by referring to characteristics of the value-added process from the utility-layer to the supply-layer and refer to this layer as the "conversion-layer". The position in the conversion layer is decided by two dimensions: The proportion of the involved substances that are recycled, and the exergy efficiency referring to the amount of useful work per cost unit.

The aim of this text has not been to call for more or less publicly provided goods. The issues included in the multi-layered approach to public goods does not determine a public sector provision or a private sector provision. The approach highlights how different categories of public goods have different characteristics – advantages and disadvantages – depending on the context. There are issues *firms* should consider when they choose or innovate a good, and when they choose how they should provide a good, while *governments* should consider how the costs of negative externalities are to be compensated: By *public* funding, based on public provision or subsidies, or by *firms* paying for the costs of their own negative externalities through a tax.

The decision of whether a public good should be provided or not, is determined by the demand expressed in the market and in the political process.[1] The best adapted category of public supply for any given good may be based on what Cowen and Sutter (1999) refer to as the "cooperative efficacy", or changes in the supply-layer that are due to changes in the level of excludability and/or rivalry ("cooperative"), and/or changes in the conversion-layer that are due to a change in the level of energy efficiency and material efficiency ("efficacy").

What do we achieve by treating public goods in this way? A multi-layered approach to public goods sheds new light on technological, economic, and institutional trends by distinguishing between the good itself, the provision of the good, and the efficiency related to the provision of the good. A multi-layered approach to public goods is shown to be useful in many different domains, but this is only a first attempt to utilize this approach. Further work on the design of public good layers and on the implications of changes within and between these layers is needed to validate the benefits of this approach.

Note

1 When the selection of the provider is based on the market demand, the role of the state is typically to introduce (dis-)incentives where the market fails to produce an optimal outcome. When the selection of the provider is based on a political process, the role of the state is typically to intervene where the market outcome results in an unacceptable distribution or if the market outcome fails to adequately protect human dignity or human rights. This mirror the categories of "Three normative models of the welfare state" in Heath (2011).

Literature

Acheson, J. M. (2015). Private land and common oceans: Analysis of the development of property regimes. *Current Anthropology, 56*(1), 28–55.

Adams, R., Bessant, J., & Phelps, R. (2006). Innovation management measurement: A review. *International Journal of Management Reviews, 8*(1), 21–47.

Adams, R. D., & McCormick, K. (1987). Private goods, club goods, and public goods as a continuum. *Review of Social Economy, 45*(2), 192–199.

Adams, R. M. (1960, September). The origin of cities. *Scientific American, 203*(3), 153–172.

Adams, R. M. (1974). Anthropological perspectives on ancient trade. *Current Anthropology, 15*(3), 239–258.

Akbar, Y. H., & Tracogna, A. (2018). The sharing economy and the future of the hotel industry: Transaction cost theory and platform economics. *International Journal of Hospitality Management, 71*, 91–101.

Alstone, P., Gershenson, D., & Kammen, D. M. (2015). Decentralized energy systems for clean electricity access. *Nature Climate Change, 5*(4), 305.

Anton, A. (2000). Public goods as common stock: Notes on the reading commons. In A. Anton, M. Fisk, & N. Holmstrom (Eds.), *Not for sale: In defense of public goods*. Boulder: Westview Press.

Ayres, R. U. (1998). Eco-thermodynamics: Economics and the second law. *Ecological Economics, 26*(2), 189–209.

Ayres, R. U. (2016). *Energy, complexity and wealth maximization*. London: Springer International Publishing.

Ayres, R. U., & Warr, B. (2009). *The economic growth engine*. Cheltenham: Edward Elgar Publishing Inc.

Bardy, R., & Massaro, M. (2013). Shifting the paradigm of return on investment: A composite index to measure overall corporate performance. *Corporate Governance, 13*(5), 498–510.

Barnett, W., & Block, W. (2007). Coase and Van Zandt on lighthouses. *Public Finance Review, 35*(6), 710–733.

Barrett, S. (2002). Supplying international public goods: How nations can cooperate, Chapter 3. In M. Ferroni & A. Mody (Eds.), *International public goods: Incentives, measurement, and financing*. Boston: Kluwer Academic Publishers and The World Bank.

Basu, S., Andrews, J., Kishore, S., Panjabi, R., & Stuckler, D. (2012). Comparative performance of private and public healthcare systems in low-and middle-income countries: A systematic review. *PLoS Medicine, 9*(6), e1001244.

Batina, R. G., & Ihori, T. (2005). *Public goods: Theories and evidence.* London: Springer Science & Business Media.

Bender, B. (1978). Gatherer-hunter to farmer: A social perspective. *World Archaeology, 10*(2), 204–222.

Bendix, R. (1977). *Nation-building and citizenship.* Berkeley: University of California Press. (First published by John Wiley & Sons, Inc. in 1964.)

Bertrand, E. (2005). The Coasean analysis of lighthouse financing: Myths and realities. *Cambridge Journal of Economics, 30*(3), 389–402.

Block, W., & Jankovic, I. (2016). Tragedy of partnerships: A critique of Elinor Ostrom. *American Journal of Economic and Sociology, 75*(2), 289–318.

Blomqvist, P. (2004). The choice revolution: Privatization of Swedish welfare services in the 1990s. *Social Policy & Administration, 38*(2), 139–155.

Boitet, C., Blanchon, H., Seligman, M., & Bellynck, V. (2010, August). *MT on and for the web.* Budapest: Natural Language Processing and Knowledge Engineering (NLP-KE), 2010 International Conference (pp. 1–10). IEEE.

Boserup, E. (1965). *The conditions of agricultural growth: The economics of agrarian change under population pressure.* London: George Allen & Unwin Ltd.

Bromley, D. W. (1989). Property relations and economic development: The other land reform. *World Development, 17*(6), 867–877.

Brown, R. E. (2008, July). *Impact of smart grid on distribution system design.* PIttsburgh: Power and Energy Society General Meeting-Conversion and Delivery of Electrical Energy in the 21st Century, 2008 IEEE (pp. 1–4). IEEE.

Buchanan, J. M. (1965). An economic theory of clubs. *Economica, 32*(125), 1–14.

Buchanan, J. M. (1968). *The demand and supply of public goods.* Chicago: Rand McNally & Company.

Candela, R. A., & Geloso, V. J. (2018). The lightship in economics. *Public Choice, 176*(3–4), 479–506.

Carbon Tax Center. (2019). Website founded by the economists Charles Komanoff and Daniel Rosenblum. The website monitors carbon tax reforms. Their staff is situated in New York/USA. Retrieved May 10, 2019, from www.carbontax.org

Childe, V. G. (1950). The urban revolution. *Town Planning Review, 21*(1), 3–17.

Chinman, M. J., & Wandersman, A. (1999). The benefits and costs of volunteering in community organizations: Review and practical implications. *Nonprofit and Voluntary Sector Quarterly, 28*(1), 46–64.

Coase, R. H. (1974). The lighthouse in economics. *Journal of Law and Economics, 17*(2), 357–376.

Cohn, G. (1895). *The science of finance.* (T. B. Veblen, Trans.). Chicago: The University of Chicago Press.

Colm, G. (1956). Comments on Samuelson's theory of public finance. *The Review of Economics and Statistics, 38*(4), 408–412.

Cornes, R., & Sandler, T. (1996). *The theory of externalities, public goods, and club goods.* Cambridge, MA: Cambridge University Press.

Cowen, T. (1985). Public goods definitions and their institutional context: A critique of public goods theory. *Review of Social Economy, 43*(1), 53–63.

Cowen, T., & Sutter, D. (1999). The costs of cooperation. *The Review of Austrian Economics, 12*(2), 161–173.

Davis, K. (1955). The origin and growth of urbanization in the world. *American Journal of Sociology, 60*(5), 429–437.

Davis, O. A., & Whinston, A. B. (1967). On the distinction between public and private goods. *The American Economic Review, 57*(2), 360–373.

Desmarais-Tremblay, M. (2014). *On the definition of public goods.* Assessing Richard A. Musgrave's contribution. CES Working Papers, Centre d'Economie de la Sorbonne. Retrieved November 10, 2018, from https://halshs.archives-ouvertes.fr/halshs-00951577/document

Doering III, O. C. (2007). The political economy of public goods: Why economists should care. *American Journal of Agricultural Economics, 89*(5), 1125–1133.

Dougherty, K. L. (2003). Public goods theory from eighteenth century political philosophy to twentieth century economics. *Public Choice, 117*(3–4), 239–253.

Eden, L., & Hampson, F. O. (1997). Clubs are trump: The formation of international regimes in the absence of a hegemon, Chapter 12. In J. R. Hollingsworth & R. Boyer (Eds.), *Contemporary capitalism: The embeddedness of institutions* (p. 361). Cambridge, MA: Cambridge University Press.

Encyclopædia Britannica. (1967). William Benton publisher (Vols. 1, Vol, 5, pp. 164–165). Chicago and London.

Farhangi, H. (2010, January–February). The path of the smart grid. *IEEE Power and Energy Magazine, 8*(1), 18–28.

Friedman, M. (1962). *Capitalism and freedom.* Chicago: University of Chicago Press.

Fukuyama, F. (2011). *The origins of political order.* London: Profile Books Ltd.

Galbraith, J. K. (1958). *The affluent society.* Boston: The Riverside Press Cambridge. Houghton Mifflin Company Books.

Gilmore, J. H., & Pine, B. J. (1997, January–February). The four faces of customization. *Harvard Business Review,* 91–101.

Gordon, R. W. (1995). Paradoxical property. In J. Brewer & S. Staves (Eds.), *Early modern conceptions of property.* London: Routledge.

The Guardian. (2018, October 26). *Canada passed a carbon tax that will give most Canadians more money.* Retrieved April 24, 2019, from www.theguardian.com/environment/climate-consensus-97-per-cent/2018/oct/26/canada-passed-a-carbon-tax-that-will-give-most-canadians-more-money

Habermas, J. (1976). *Legitimation crisis.* Translated from the German edition (1973) by Thomas McCarthy. London: Heinemann Educational Books Ltd.

Hammond, G. P., & Stapleton, A. J. (2001). Exergy analysis of the United Kingdom energy system. Proceedings of the institution of mechanical engineers, Part A. *Journal of Power and Energy, 215*(2), 141–162.

Hardin, G. (1968). The tragedy of the commons. *Science, 162,* 1243–1248.

Harvey, J., Smith, A., & Golightly, D. (2018). Online technology as a driver of sharing. In P. A. Albinsson & B. Y. Perera (Eds.), *The rise of the sharing economy: Exploring the challenges and opportunities of collaborative consumption* (pp. 75–96). Santa Barbara, CA: Praeger.

Hayami, Y., & Godo, Y. (2005). *Development economics: From the poverty to the wealth of nations*. Oxford, UK: Oxford University Press.

Hayek, F. A. (1944). *The road to serfdom*. Abingdon, UK: George Routledge & Sons.

Hayek, F. A. (1988). *The Fatal Conceit: The Errors of Socialism*. In The Collected Works of FA Hayek, WW Bartley, ed. Chicago: University of Chicago.

Head, J. G. (1962). Public-goods and public-policy. *Public Finance-Finances Publiques, 17*(3), 197–219.

Heath, J. (2011). Three normative models of the welfare state. *Public Reason, 3*(2), 13–43.

Henderson, R. M., & Clark, K. B. (1990). Architectural innovation: The reconfiguration of existing. *Administrative science quarterly, 35*(1), 9–30.

Hill, P. (1999). Tangibles, intangibles and services: A new taxonomy for the classification of output. *The Canadian Journal of Economics/Revue Canadienne d'Economique, 32*(2), 426–446.

Hira, A., & Reilly, K. (2017). The emergence of the sharing economy: Implications for development. *Journal of Developing Societies, 33*(2), 175–190.

Hole, F. (1984). A reassessment of the Neolithic revolution. *Paléorient, 10*(2), 49–60. Retrieved November 7, 2017, from www.jstor.org/stable/41489605

Holtermann, S. E. (1972). Externalities and public goods. *Economica, 39*(153), 78–87.

Hopkinson, P., Zils, M., Hawkins, P., & Roper, S. (2018). Managing a complex global circular economy business model: Opportunities and challenges. *California Management Review, 60*(3), 71–94.

Hoppe, H. (2007). Capitalist production and the problem of public goods (excerpt), Chapter 6. In E. P. Springham (Ed.), *Anarchy and the law: The political economy of choice* (pp. 107–126). Oakland, CA: The Independent Institute.

Hsu, J. (2010). *The relative efficiency of public and private service delivery*. World Health Report Background Paper, 39, pp. 1–9.

Hume, D. (1888). *A treatise of human nature*. Oxford: Clarendon Press. (Reprinted from the original edition.)

Kahneman, D., & Knetsch, J. L. (1992). Valuing public goods: The purchase of moral satisfaction. *Journal of Environmental Economics and Management, 22*(1), 57–70.

Kakran, S., & Chanana, S. (2018). Smart operations of smart grids integrated with distributed generation: A review. *Renewable and Sustainable Energy Reviews, 81*, 524–535.

Katila, R. (2007). *Measuring innovation performance*, Chapter 14. In A. Neely (Ed.), *Business performance measurement*. Cambridge, MA: Cambridge University Press.

Kaul, I. (2010). Collective self-interest. *The Broker*, Issue 20–21.

Kaul, I., & Mendoza, R. U. (2003). Advancing the concept of public goods. In I. Kaul, P. Conceicao, K. Le Goulven, & R. U. Mendoza (Eds.), *Providing global public goods: Managing globalization* (pp. 78–98). Oxford, UK: Oxford University Press.

Knoke, D. (1988). Incentives in collective action organizations. *American Sociological Review*, 311–329.

Koukal, B. (2017). *Airbnb: Growth and market share*. Blog text on his own site. Retrieved October 22, 2018, from http://kookie.cz/ilovedata/2017/08/06/airbnb-growth-and-market-share/

Kümmel, R. (2011). *The second law of economics*. Würzburg: Springer.

Landsbankinn Economic Research. (2017). *Growth seeking balance – Economic analysis of tourism in Iceland*. Retrieved October 27, 2017, from www.lands bankinn.is/Uploads/Documents/Hagsja/2017-10-11_Tourism.pdf

Lane, J. E. (1993). *The public sector: Concepts, models and approaches*. London: Sage Publications Ltd.

Laudal, T. (2018). Measuring shared value in multinational corporations. *Social Responsibility Journal, 14*(4), 917–933.

Ledyard, J. O. (1994). *Public goods: A survey of experimental research*, Social science working paper 861. Pasadena: California Institute of Technology. Retrieved October 27, 2017, from http://pascal.iseg.utl.pt/~depeco/summer school2007/9405003.pdf

Light, A. (2000). Public goods, future generations and environmental quality. In A. Anton, M. Fisk, & N. Holmstom (Eds.), *Not for sale: In defense of public goods* (pp. 209–225). Boulder/Colorado: Westview Press.

Lindblom, C. E. (1977). *Politics and markets: The world's political-economic systems*. New York: Basic Books.

Lively, J. (1975). *Democracy*. Oxford: John Wiley & Sons Ltd.

Lloyd, W. F. (1832). *Two lectures on the checks to population delivered to the University of Oxford*. Printed by S. Collingwood, printer to the University for the author. Retrieved May 8, 2019, from https://philosophy.lander.edu/intro/artic les/lloyd_commons.pdf

Malkin, J., & Wildavsky, A. (1991). Why the traditional distinction between public and private goods should be abandoned. *Journal of Theoretical Politics, 3*(4), 355–378.

Manthorpe, R. (2018, February 2). Airbnb is taking over London – and this data proves it. *Wired Magazine*. Retrieved October 22, 2018, from www.wired.co. uk/article/airbnb-growth-london-housing-data-insideairbnb

Marginson, S. (2016). Public/private in higher education: A synthesis of economic and political approaches. *Studies in Higher Education*, 1–16.

Mercier, H., & Sperber, D. (2017). *The enigma of reason*. Cambridge, MA: Harvard University Press.

Mill, J. S. (1861). *Considerations on representative government*. London: Parker, Son, and Bourn, West Strand.

Mukand, S. W., & Rodrik, D. (2017). *The political economy of liberal democracy*, CESifo Working Paper, No. 6433, Center for Economic Studies and ifo Institute (CESifo), Munchen. Retrieved April 25, 2019, from www.econstor.eu/handle/ 10419/161872

Musgrave, R. A., & Musgrave, P. B. (1973). *Public finance in theory and practice*. New York: McGraw-Hill Education.

Nepal, R., & Jamasb, T. (2015). Caught between theory and practice: Government, market, and regulatory failure in electricity sector reforms. *Economic Analysis and Policy, 46*, 16–24.

Neto, J. Q. F., Walther, G., Bloemhof, J. A. E. E., Van Nunen, J. A. E. E., & Spengler, T. (2010). From closed-loop to sustainable supply chains: The WEEE case. *International Journal of Production Research*, *48*(15), 4463–4481.

Oakland, W. H. (1969). Joint goods. *Economica*, *36*(143), 253–268.

OECD. (2017a). Health expenditure and financing: Health expenditure indicators. *OECD Health Statistics*. Retrieved October 27, 2017, from http://dx.doi.org/10.1787/data-00349-en

OECD. (2017b). Inflation (CPI) (indicator). Retrieved October 27, 2017, from https://data.oecd.org/chart/4Z2i

OECD. (2017c). *Education at a glance 2017: OECD indicators*. Paris: OECD Publishing. Retrieved April 10, 2019 from http://dx.doi.org/10.1787/eag-2017-en

OECD. (2017d). *State of higher education 2015–16: OECD higher education program*. Retrieved October 27, 2017, from www.oecd.org/edu/imhe/The%20State%20of%20Higher%20Education%202015-16.pdf

Olson, M. (1971). *The logic of collective action: Public goods and the theory of groups*. Cambridge, MA: Harvard University Press. (First print published in 1965.)

Ostrom, E. (1990). *Governing the commons: The evolution of institutions for collective action*. Cambridge: Cambridge University Press.

Ostrom, E., & Ostrom, V. (1977). *Public economy organization and service delivery*. Paper presented at the Workshop in political theory and political analysis at the University of Michigan. Retrieved October 27, 2017, from https://dlc.dlib.indiana.edu/dlc/bitstream/handle/10535/732/ostrom01.pdf?sequence=1

O'Sullivan, A. (2006). The first cities. In R. J. Arnott & D. P. McMillen (Eds.), *A companion to urban economics*. Oxford: Blackwell Publishing Ltd. doi:10.1002/9780470996225.ch3

Pateman, C. (1970). *Participation and democratic theory*. Cambridge: Cambridge University Press.

Peters, J. S., Brewer, J., & Staves, S. (1996). *Early modern conceptions of property*. London: Routledge.

Pine II, B. J (1993). *Mass customization: The new frontier in business competition*. Boston: Harvard Business School Press.

Pine II, B. J., Victor, B., & Boynton, A. C. (1993). Making mass customization work. Harvard Business Review, *71*(5), 108–111.

Polanyi, K. (1944). *The great transformation* (Vol. 2, p. 145). Boston: Beacon Press.

Porter, M. E. (1980). *Competitive strategy: Techniques for analyzing industries and competitors*. New York: The Free Press.

Porter, M. E., & Kramer, M. R. (2011). Creating shared value. *Harvard Business Review, 89*(1–2), 62–77.

Radin, M. J. (1987). Market-inalienability. *Harvard Law Review, 100*(8), 1849–1937.

Rege, M., & Telle, K. (2004). The impact of social approval and framing on cooperation in public good situations. *Journal of Public Economics, 88*(7), 1625–1644.

Richard, B., & Cleveland, S. (2016). The future of hotel chains: Branded marketplaces driven by the sharing economy. *Journal of Vacation Marketing, 22*(3), 239–248.

Rifkin, J. (2014). *The zero marginal cost society*. New York: Palgrave Macmillan and St. Martin's Press LLC.

Rivers, N. (2014). *The case for a carbon tax in Canada*. Canada 2020. Retrieved April 24, 209, from http://canada2020.ca/wp-content/uploads/2014/11/The-Case-for-a-Carbon-Tax-in-Canada.pdf

Rosen, M. A. (2005, March–April). *Exergy*. Published in "Canadian Consulting Engineer". Retrieved October 27, 2017, from www.canadianconsultingengineer.com/features/exergy/

Rowley, J. (2006). An analysis of the e-service literature: Towards a research agenda. *Internet Research, 16*(3), 339–359.

Samuelson, P. A. (1948). *Economics: An introductory analysis*. New York: McGraw-Hill.

Samuelson, P. A. (1954). The pure theory of public expenditure. *The Review of Economics and Statistics, 36*(4), 387–389.

Samuelson, P. A. (1964). *Economics: An introductory analysis* (6th ed.). London: McGraw Hill.

Saraswat, S., Gupta, H. P., & Dutta, T. (2018, January). *Fog based energy efficient ubiquitous systems*. Bengaluru: Communication Systems & Networks (COMS-NETS), 2018 10th International Conference (pp. 439–442). IEEE.

Saussier, J. (2015, November 15). Sharing as a distruptive force. *Global Investor* (2).

Scanlon, K., Whitehead, C., & Arrigoitia, M. F. (Eds.). (2014). *Social housing in Europe*. Hoboken, NJ: John Wiley & Sons.

Schumpeter, J. A. (1939). *Business cycles: A theoretical, historical and statistical analysis of the capitalist process*. New York: McGraw-Hill Book Company.

Schumpeter, J. A. (1942). *Capitalism, socialism and democracy*. New York: Routledge.

Sikorski, J. J., Haughton, J., & Kraft, M. (2017). Blockchain technology in the chemical industry: Machine-to-machine electricity market. *Applied Energy, 195,* 234–246.

Silva, B. N., Khan, M., & Han, K. (2018). Towards sustainable smart cities: A review of trends, architectures, components, and open challenges in smart cities. *Sustainable Cities and Society, 38*, 697–713.

Simula, H. (2007). *Concept of innovation revisited – A framework for a product innovation*. Miami Beach: International Association for Management of Technology IAMOT 2007 Proceedings.

Smith, K. (2005). Measuring innovation. In J. Fagerberg, D. C. Mowery, & R. R. Nelson (Eds.), *The Oxford handbook of innovation*. Oxford: Oxford University Press.

Solstad, J. T., & Brekke, K. A. (2011). Does the existence of a public good enhance cooperation among users of common-pool resources? *Land Economics, 87*(2), 335–345.

Srivastava, S. K. (2007). Green supply-chain management: A state-of-the-art literature review. *International Journal of Management Reviews, 9*(1), 53–80.

Starr, P. (1988). The meaning of privatization. *Yale Law & Policy Review, 6*(1), 6–41.

Stiglitz, J. E. (1982). *The theory of local public goods twenty-five years after Tiebout: A perspective*, Working paper No. 954 in the NBER Working paper series. Retrieved April 23, 2019, from www.nber.org/papers/w0954.pdf

Stretton, H., & Orchard, L. (1994). *Public goods, public enterprise, public choice.* London: The Macmillan Press Ltd.

Sturn, R. (2010). 'Public goods' before Samuelson: Interwar Finanzwissenschaft and Musgrave's synthesis. *The European Journal of the History of Economic Thought, 17*(2), 279–312.

Svanborg-Sjövall, K. (2014). Privatising the Swedish welfare state. *Economic Affairs, 34*(2), 181–192.

Thurow, L. (1996). *The future of capitalism.* New York: Penguin Books.

Tiebout, C. M. (1956). A pure theory of local expenditures. *Journal of Political Economy, 64*(5), 416–424.

Toucqueville, A. de (1848). *Democracy in America.* (H. Reeve, Trans.), ESQ from French text first published in 1835. New York: Pratt Woodford, & Co.

Tourism Review. (2017, May 29). *The market share of airbnb in the Netherlands rising sharply.* . Retrieved November 13, 2017, from www.tourism-review.com/airbnb-in-the-netherlands-highly-popular-news5416

Trivedi, P., & Sagar, K. K. (2010). Emerging trends of ubiquitous computing. *International Journal of Advanced Computer Science and Applications, 1*(3), 72–74.

Tufis, D. (2014, September 18–19). *Machine translation a look into the future.* Conference Linguistic Resources and Tools for Processing the Romania Language (p. 19).

Unruh, G. (2018). Circular economy, 3D printing, and the biosphere rules. *California Management Review, 60*(3), 95–111.

Usher, A. P. (1954). *A history of mechanical innovations.* Berkeley, MA: Harvard University Press.

Van Zandt, D. E. (1993). The lessons of the lighthouse: "Government" or "private" provision of goods. *The Journal of Legal Studies, 22*(1), 47–72.

Vandevelde, K. J. (1980). The new property of the nineteenth century: The development of the modern concept of property. *Buffalo Law Review, 29*, 325–367.

Ver Eecke, W. (1999). Public goods: An ideal concept. *The Journal of Socio-Economics, 28*(2), 139–156.

Vingerhoets, P., Chebbo, M., & Hatziargyriou, N. (2016). *The digital energy system 4.0.* Report published by Smartgrids, receiving funding from the European Commission. Retrieved November 2018, from www.etip-snet.eu/wp-content/uploads/2017/04/ETP-SG-Digital-Energy-System-4.0-2016.pdf

Weiser, M. (1991, September). The computer for the 21st century. *Scientific American 265*(3), 94–105.

Wolsink, M. (2012). The research agenda on social acceptance of distributed generation in smart grids: Renewable as common pool resources. *Renewable and Sustainable Energy Reviews, 16*(1), 822–835.

Wörner, D., Von Bomhard, T., Schreier, Y.-P., & Bilgeri, D. (2016). *The bitcoin ecosystem: Disruption beyond financial services?* Research Paper. 33 to the ECIS 2016 Proceedings. Retrieved April 30, 2019, from http://aisel.aisnet.org/ecis2016_rp/33

Appendix

Suggested positions of goods in the utility-layer and supply-layer

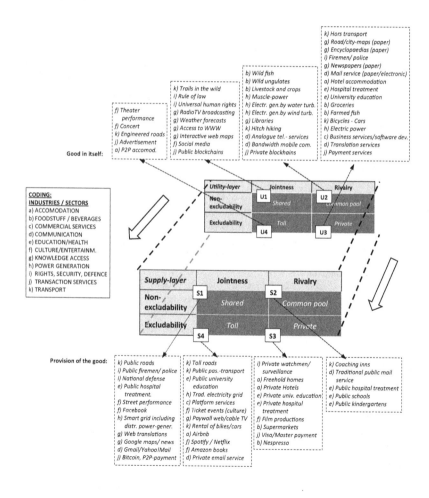

Suggested positions of public goods in the utility-layer and the supply-layer

This monograph refers only to a sample of these public goods. The positioning of goods in this annex is only tentative with the aim of stimulating debate.

Index

Note: Numbers in italics indicate figures and in bold indicate tables on the corresponding pages.

Printed in the United States
by Baker & Taylor Publisher Services